E. W. Brabrook

Provident Societies and Industrial Welfare

Elibron Classics
www.elibron.com

Elibron Classics series.

ISBN 1-4021-4828-3 (paperback)
ISBN 1-4212-7644-5 (hardcover)

This Elibron Classics Replica Edition is an unabridged facsimile of the edition published in 1898 by Blackie & Son, Limited, London.

Published monthly.

The

Victorian Era Series.

In crown 8vo volumes, cloth, 2*s.* 6*d.* each.

The series is designed to form a record of the great movements and developments of the age, in politics, economics, religion, industry, literature, science, and art, and of the life work of its typical and influential men.

Under the general editorship of Mr. J. HOLLAND ROSE, M.A., late Scholar of Christ's College, Cambridge, the individual volumes will be contributed by leading specialists in the various branches of knowledge which fall to be treated in the series.

Already published.

The Rise of Democracy.
By J. HOLLAND ROSE, M.A.

The Anglican Revival.
By J. H. OVERTON, D.D., Canon of Lincoln.

John Bright.
By C. A. VINCE, M.A., late Fellow of Christ's College, Cambridge.

Charles Dickens. By GEORGE GISSING.

The Growth and Administration of the British Colonies, 1837–1897.
By the Rev. W. P. GRESWELL, M.A., author of "Africa South of the Zambesi", "History of the Dominion of Canada".

The Free-trade Movement and its Results.

By G. ARMITAGE-SMITH, M.A., Principal of the Birkbeck Institution, and for many years Lecturer on Economics for the London Society for the Extension of University Teaching.

English National Education.

By H. HOLMAN, M.A., formerly Professor of Education in the University College of Wales, Aberystwyth.

Provident Societies and Industrial Welfare.

By E. W. BRABROOK, C.B., Chief Registrar of Friendly Societies.

Forthcoming volumes—

The Growth of London, 1837–1897.

By G. LAURENCE GOMME.

Charles Kingsley and the Christian Social Movement.

By the Very Rev. C. W. STUBBS, D.D., Dean of Ely.

Recent Advances in Astronomy.

By A. H. FISON, D.Sc. (Lond.).

The Science of Life. By J. ARTHUR THOMSON, M.A.

Indian Life and Thought since the Mutiny.

By R. P. KARKARIA, B.A., Principal of the New Collegiate Institution, Bombay, and Examiner in History and Philosophy to the University of Bombay.

Alfred, Lord Tennyson: A CRITICAL STUDY.

By STEPHEN GWYNN.

British Foreign Missions.

By Rev. WARDLAW THOMPSON and Rev. A. N. JOHNSON, M.A.

*** *Prospectus and press opinions may be had on application.*

LONDON: BLACKIE & SON, LIMITED, 50 OLD BAILEY, E.C.
GLASGOW, AND DUBLIN.

The Victorian Era Series

Provident Societies and Industrial Welfare

Provident Societies

and

Industrial Welfare

By

E. W. BRABROOK, C.B.
Chief Registrar of Friendly Societies

LONDON
BLACKIE & SON, LIMITED, 50 OLD BAILEY, E.C.
GLASGOW AND DUBLIN
1898

Preface

The general object and scope of this work are fully explained in Chapter I. The large share which Provident Societies have had in the promotion of Industrial Welfare during the Victorian Era is worthy of even ampler record. Those who desire to pursue the subject in further detail may find means of doing so in the Guide Book of the Friendly Societies' Registry Office, the Annual Reports since 1855 of the Registrar, and since 1875 of the Chief Registrar of Friendly Societies, the Parliamentary Returns of Building Societies, and the Labour Gazette and other publications of the Board of Trade relating to Trade-Unions.

Contents

Contents

Provident Societies and Industrial Welfare.

Chapter I.

Introductory.

It is the good fortune of the writer to have been associated for nearly thirty years with a public department that exists for the benefit of the industrial population. There is no act it does that is not the conferring of a privilege. The bodies with which it has to deal claim its services at their own option. Any one of them might dispense with those services if it cared to do so. As the subject of the present volume is almost wholly limited to the institutions which hold a relation of one kind or another to the Registry of Friendly Societies, it may be worth while to state at the outset, in general terms, what are the history and principal functions of that department. Its existence in its present form belongs wholly to the Victorian Era.

From 1828 to 1846 a number of important duties had been devolved by statute upon a barrister appointed by the Commissioners for the Reduction of the National Debt. An act of 1828 gave him the examination and certifying of the rules of savings-banks. These had formerly been submitted for the approval of the justices at Quarter Sessions. An act of 1829 gave him the examination and certifying of the rules of Friendly Societies. These functions were purely legal; but as it was very desirable in the interests of Friendly Societies that correct information as to the rates of sickness and mortality should be obtained, it was provided that every society should, after its rules had been certified, send to the barrister every five years a return of its experience, and that he should lay an abstract of the returns before Parliament. The first such abstract was made in 1835. The legislature attached so much importance to these functions of the barrister in question, and was so desirous to facilitate his labours, that it was enacted in 1834 that letters to and from him should be free of postage. As that was before the days of Rowland Hill, it was an important concession to those who had to correspond with the barrister, and a great assistance to him in the execution of his duties.

In 1835 an act was passed for the regulation of Loan Societies, and the examination and certifying of the rules of these societies was confided to the same barrister. Again, in 1836 an act was passed for the encouragement and protection of Benefit Building Societies, and the same functions were allotted to him in respect of the rules of these societies. Shortly after the accession of Her Majesty, an act was passed, exempting societies for purposes of literature, science, and the fine arts exclusively, from the payment of local rates. This privilege was not to be obtained by any such society until its rules had been submitted to the same barrister, and he had given a certificate that the society was one entitled to the benefit of the act.

This curious accumulation upon one man, in successive sessions of Parliament, of a variety of duties, seems to indicate that at that period there was much activity in the formation of societies having various praiseworthy objects, and that the person who happened to have been appointed the barrister for certifying savings-banks was a man possessing special qualifications to deal with work of the kind. It is not far from the truth to say that the legislature had been learning from experience that the best service it could render to such societies was to pass their rules under the eye of a person skilled in the art of expressing in clear and simple language the legal conditions upon which the members of associations were to be allowed to combine for beneficial purposes. It may equally justly be inferred that the creation of these several offices, and the appointment of Mr. John Tidd Pratt to fill them, were coincidences tending greatly to the public advantage.

In addition to all these functions, he was the standing counsel to the Commissioners for the Reduction of the National Debt, a body consisting of high officers of state and magnates of finance, which had originally been created to supervise the operations of the sinking fund, by which Mr. Pitt fondly hoped the national debt would be greatly reduced and in time extinguished. The Savings-bank Act of 1817, which required the deposits of savings-banks to be paid into a savings-bank fund opened at the Banks of England and Ireland, created a new sphere of duty for the commissioners, who were thereby intrusted with some control over savings-banks and with the investment of the deposits, and these new duties have since more fully engaged them than those from which they derive their name.

Mr. Pratt's functions in regard to savings-banks extended over all three parts of the United Kingdom. In regard to Loan Societies, Scotland and Ireland were excluded from the operation of the act; in regard to the other classes of societies that have been mentioned, there was a separate advocate appointed by the Lord Advocate for Scotland, and a separate barrister appointed by the Attorney-General for Ireland. The number of such societies formed in Scotland and Ireland was, however, small in comparison with those formed in England, and the gentlemen who held the appointments in these countries have not attached their names to the history of provident movements to anything like the extent which their English colleague was able to do by the variety of his functions and his interesting personality.

For a society to be "certified by Tidd Pratt" was for a long time a kind of hall-mark of respectability in the eye of many people in various parts of the country, and the name of Tidd Pratt was held up as a terror to managers suspected of evil designs, who were told "Tidd Pratt will never allow you to do this", or "if you do this, you will have Tidd Pratt upon you". The gentleman who acquired this wide-spread influence was short and thin, walked somewhat lame, had an animated manner and brilliant eyes, and impressed all with whom he came in contact with a sense of ability and *savoir faire.* He had strong convictions and was earnest in the expression of them, and brought a wide range of knowledge and experience to the performance of his duties.

Many a well-meaning person who came with the outline of a scheme which he desired to carry into effect under one or other of the many acts which Mr. Pratt administered, or who was anxious to introduce reforms into some existing society, but did not know how to set about it, found a valuable and unexpected ally in the barrister, who in a few words would direct him in the right path to accomplish what he wished. While in this respect he was something more than the dry and cold official, in other ways he was a man of wide sympathies. He was one of the founders of the Reform Club, a trustee of the Soane Museum, a fellow of the Society of Antiquaries and of the Royal Society of Literature, an honorary fellow of the Institute of Actuaries, a director of an important insurance company, and active in many other pursuits. He was author of a history of Savings-banks, a treatise on the law of Friendly Societies, a work on the Highways Acts, which is still the foundation of the standard work on that subject, and a considerable number of other books, mainly relating to branches of the law which were more or less closely connected with his functions in certifying rules.

He would not have been the man he was, however, if he had succeeded in pleasing everybody. There was one class of Friendly Society, the members of which always looked upon him as out of sympathy with their operations, and, in consequence, charged him with a degree of active obstruction to them, which probably did not exist in his intention so fully as they thought it did, and certainly was not manifested to that extent. The societies referred to are the affiliated orders which, as we shall see later on in this volume, have been growing in strength and influence of late years very considerably. They were ignored by the legislature until 1850, and, when recognized, it was in so unsatisfactory a manner that they awarded to the executive officer of the law a large share of the blame that belonged to the legislature itself. It is quite possible that, as he had for twenty-two years been the administrator of a law which ignored these societies, his sympathies were more in touch with societies of another class, and he may have held some notions which are now heterodox as to the possible dangers of large affiliated organizations, but in the business of certifying rules he could only do what the statute told him.

Such was the barrister who, at the time of the accession of Queen Victoria, had already been for nine years engaged in the interesting and useful functions which we have enumerated, and whose zeal and ability in the performance of them had led to their successive extension to one and another sort of institution connected more or less closely with the industrial classes. At that time, however, whenever he certified rules for a society, he retained no transcript of them (except in certain cases where three copies were sent to him), but returned the original to the society, and sent the duplicate for registry to some public authority, in most cases the Clerk of the Peace, so that inconvenience arose when he had to perform any subsequent act in respect of the same society, as, for example, receiving quinquennial returns—he could not tell what societies ought to send them to him.

In 1846 the legislature remedied this inconvenience by an enactment creating the barrister the head of a department, under the style of Registrar of Friendly Societies, and requiring the several Clerks of the Peace to take off their rolls the various sets of rules that he had sent to them, and to return them to him, to be kept and registered by him. In addition to the documents which he had himself sent to them, the Clerks of the Peace were required to send him all the transcripts of rules which had come into their custody between 1793 and 1828, when rules of societies were laid before the

Justices in Quarter Sessions to be examined and allowed by them, and were afterwards enrolled among the records of the Court. These were directed to be taken off the file and transmitted to the Registrar.

The result was that a vast mass of documents, most of them parchment enrolments, very unwieldy in shape and size, was sent to him from all parts of the country, and had to be registered and catalogued by him. The total number of documents appears to have amounted to about 30,000—20,000 rules of societies and 10,000 amendments of rules—so great, even at that early date, had been the progress of Friendly Societies. It should be observed that this Act of 1846 transferred to Mr. Pratt, as Registrar of Friendly Societies, only those functions which had formerly been performed by him under the Friendly Societies Acts. He still remained the barrister (not the registrar) for the purpose of Savings Banks, Loan Societies, Benefit Building Societies, and Scientific and Literary Societies. The records of these societies remained with the National Debt Commissioners or the Clerks of the Peace, as the case required.

In regard to Friendly Societies, the act conferred upon him somewhat extensive powers. He was authorized to transfer the property of a society from an incapable or absent trustee, and thus to save it the expense and worry of proceedings in Equity; to settle disputes, and for that purpose to require the production of documents and to administer oaths. He thus became a judicial officer with powers sufficient to enable him to do justice at a minimum of cost to the parties. In addition to the quinquennial returns already mentioned, every society was to send to him a report of its assets and liabilities. This provision, however, never came into operation, for before the first quinquennial period had expired, the Act of 1846 was repealed, and a consolidating act passed, in which this provision was not re-enacted. Later on, in the chapter relating to Friendly Societies, we shall have occasion to show how much this is to be regretted.

The specialization of his work still continued. In 1852 a new class of societies, the Industrial and Provident, usually known as Co-operative Societies, called for legislative encouragement and regulation, and these were confided to the Registrar of Friendly Societies. Some of them had already been registered by him under the Friendly Societies Acts as societies for the frugal investment of savings. Successive acts varied the provisions of the several statutes that have been mentioned, mostly in the direction of increasing the responsibility of the registrar or barrister, and adding new functions to those already exercised by him; but it is hardly necessary here to mention them, as we shall have to deal with them in detail under the heads of the several classes of societies to which they relate.

It should, however, be stated that the Friendly Societies Act of 1855 required the registrar to make an annual report to parliament, and from that date to the present a yearly blue-book has been issued. Mr. Pratt availed himself of the opportunity of this annual report to draw public attention to the mischievous operation of the collecting burial societies and the expensiveness of their management. He also took occasion, whenever the necessity arose, to inform the public, through the *Times* newspaper, of any facts that came to his knowledge relating to schemes tending to deceive or defraud the unwary, and was successful in prosecuting some such schemes. In one amusing case, an insurance society was started by domestic servants, who issued an attractive prospectus, in which they were described as "esquires".

It will be gathered from all that has been said that this excellent public servant fulfilled the duties confided to him with great zeal and efficiency. Early in 1869 his health began to fail, and the writer, who had then recently been called to the bar, was appointed to assist him. Mr. Pratt died in January, 1870, having completed forty-one years' public service. At the time of his death, the Right Hon. Robert Lowe was Chancellor of the Exchequer, and in that capacity would have had the right to fill up the vacant office; but he formed the opinion that it was not desirable to continue the Registry of Friendly Societies, and introduced a bill into parliament to transfer its functions to other departments. He advocated this course on the ground that the certificate of the registrar had been misunderstood.

It was found, however, necessary that the office should be filled up, at least temporarily, and the Assistant Solicitor to the Treasury, now Sir Augustus Stephenson, was requested to perform the necessary duties in the interval before the abolition of the Department. Meanwhile, some of the societies concerned made representations to the government, which induced them to think that further inquiry would be desirable before the bill was proceeded with. Accordingly, a Royal Commission was appointed, of which Sir Stafford Northcote (afterwards Earl of Iddesleigh) was chairman. Of the other members of the Commission, Sir Michael Hicks-Beach, Sir Sydney Waterlow, and Mr. C. S. Roundell, M.P., are now the only survivors. Mr. J. M. Ludlow was the secretary to the Commission. Other members were Mr. J. Bonham Carter, M.P., Mr. E. M.

Richards, M.P., Mr. F. T. Bircham, solicitor, and Mr. W. P. Pattison, actuary—all since deceased.

They were directed "to inquire into the existing state of the law relating to Friendly Societies, and to inquire into and report upon the operation of the acts relating to Friendly Societies and Benefit Building Societies, and the organization or general condition of societies established under such acts respectively, and upon the office and duties of the Registrar of Friendly Societies, with power to suggest improvements in the law". They entered upon this comprehensive inquiry in 1870, and did not complete it until 1874. In 1871 they obtained power to appoint Assistant-Commissioners, and these gentlemen—the Hon. E. Lyulph Stanley, Sir George Young, Mr. E. Lynch Daniell, and Mr. G. Culley—visited various parts of the country, and presented reports on the condition of the Friendly Societies in the districts allotted to them, comprising a great body of valuable information.

The fourth and final report of the Royal Commission was a document filling 216 folio pages and containing 931 numbered paragraphs. It summed up their chief recommendations under 46 heads, some of which were adopted by the legislature. Among these were, that the registration of Friendly Societies should continue, the second report having recommended that Building Societies should be registered. Meanwhile, the legislature itself had continued the previous practice of intrusting new duties to the registrar. In 1871 Trade-unions were legalized, and the functions of registering their rules, receiving annual returns from them, and publishing an abstract of such returns, were imposed upon the registrar. An amending act in 1876 materially increased his powers with regard to those bodies.

In 1874 the enrolment of Benefit Building Societies, which had commenced in 1836, was abolished, and the Clerks of the Peace were directed to send the rules and other documents in their custody to the registrar; future Building Societies were to be incorporated by his certificate and the rules registered by him, and many new functions were imposed upon him in respect to such societies.

In 1875 an act was passed, by which some of the recommendations of the Royal Commission were carried into effect. A central office was created, consisting of a Chief Registrar, and one or more Assistant Registrars in London, with Assistant Registrars in Scotland and Ireland, and a complete actuarial staff. Previously the registrars in the three parts of the United Kingdom had been independent. The functions of the registrar of Friendly Societies and of the barrister to certify the rules of Savings-banks were consolidated, and the law was amended in many other respects. A few more clauses would have made the consolidation more effectual, and removed some anomalies that still exist, but opposition to them was raised, and the legislature could not be prevailed upon to adopt them.

Early in 1875 Mr. Stephenson, Assistant Solicitor to the Treasury, became the Solicitor to the Treasury, and resigned the office of registrar. Mr. John Malcolm Ludlow, Secretary to the Royal Commission, which had then completed its labours, was appointed registrar and barrister to certify, and later in the year, when the Act of 1875 was passed, became the first chief registrar. The Commissioners, in their report, had recorded their "very strong sense of the important services rendered, not so much to themselves as to the public, by Mr. Ludlow, who had throughout their proceedings taken by far the largest share of the labour of the Commission, and but for whose devotion to the work they would have felt themselves unable to deal in a comprehensive manner with the numerous and complicated questions involved. Mr. Ludlow's great knowledge of, and interest in, the subject had made his assistance unusually valuable, and if the report should be found to contain a more complete account of the great system of Friendly Societies, and of the questions involved in their management and regulation, and their various relations to the community, than had yet been given to the public, it would be to the exertions of Mr. Ludlow, more than of any other individual, that this result would be due."

Mr. Ludlow had, however, many years before, established a high claim on the gratitude and confidence of the industrial community. By his labours with F. D. Maurice and others in the cause of popular education, and with E. V. Neale, Charles Kingsley, Thomas Hughes, and others in the cause of industrial co-operation, and by the enlightened support and sympathy he had given to the cause of Trade-unions, he had marked himself out as the fittest man for the exercise of functions for which a deep knowledge of the sentiments of the working-classes, and a cordial desire to help them, are qualifications of primary importance. It was under these inspirations that Mr. Ludlow fulfilled his duties until 1891, when he retired from office, leaving to his successor an easy task in the maintenance of the good feeling that he had established between the registry office and the various classes of societies with which it has to deal.

Since his retirement from the office of chief registrar, Mr. Ludlow has continued to serve the public as a member of the Inspection Committee of Trustee Savings, banks, a body which has done much to prevent the recurrence of those frauds and irregularities in savings-bank management which have in past times greatly injured the cause of thrift.

The legislature has continued to find new functions for the activity of the Registry Office, and hardly a year has passed of late in which some enactment has not been made extending its powers or imposing upon it new responsibilities and new duties, to be exercised either in a judicial, executive, or discretionary manner. Among these may be mentioned the extended authority over Building Societies, conferred by the Act of 1894, under which the registrar is enabled to direct inquiry into their management and inspection of their books, to cancel their registry and compulsorily to wind them up, if occasion should arise and the conditions precedent stated in the act had been fulfilled.

Still more noteworthy is the authority given to the registrar under the Workman's Compensation Act 1897 to certify schemes entered into by employers and workmen for contracting out of the provisions of that act, in which a very wide discretion is left to the registrar in granting certificates, and extensive powers of investigation and of cancelling certificates, are contained.

One other observation may be made as to the registry of Friendly Societies. While it is a Government department, it is not the depositary of any state secrets. On the contrary, it is enjoined by statute to publish and circulate, or otherwise make known, such information useful to the members of, or to persons interested in, societies registered, or capable of being registered, as the chief registrar may think fit. The present publication is not, of course, one made under the authority of the act, but the writer hopes that it may serve the same excellent purpose, and has been induced to prepare it by the feeling that the unofficial comments of an independent but friendly observer may possibly be useful and interesting, not only to those members and other persons whose advantage the act has in contemplation, but to those of the public generally, to whom information as to the great extent and the beneficial operation of Provident Societies and their bearing on industrial welfare has not before been offered.

Chapter II.

Trade-Unions.

If we seek to place ourselves in the position of a member of the industrial population, at the outset of life, well-disposed and well-informed, anxious to do the best he can for his own interests in the present and in the future, we shall probably find, if he belongs to a trade which is organized, that he will think it worth while to join the organization of his trade by becoming a member of a Trade-union. It is possible that the trade may be so completely organized that he will have no option in the matter, and will not be permitted to work at it while he remains outside the Union; that is to say, that the Union will be in a position to exercise an influence powerful enough to prevent its members from working with him, and his employers from continuing him in their employment.

Even if that be not so, it is probable that he would arrive at the conviction that it is better for him and for all his comrades that he should join them in an organization which is intended to enable them to meet the employer on equal terms, and to use the powerful influence of combination to secure for the general body of workmen that which they think is for their benefit.

The question arises, however, Is a Trade-union a provident society? If not, we have no concern with it here. In a discussion on the subject before the Royal Statistical Society in April, 1895, Mr. A. H. Bailey, a distinguished actuary, said Trade-unions were not provident institutions. In this we cannot but think he took too narrow a view of what constitutes a provident institution. If a society which enables you to devote a portion of your wages towards providing for the future is a provident institution, a combination which has the object of seeing that you get sufficient wages to pay your contributions to that society must also be provident. Apart from this, Trade-unions do, to a large extent, make provision against sickness, accident, and old age.

Trade-unions are institutions of great antiquity. The trade guilds of the middle ages were trade-unions. They are now represented in London by the wealthy city companies, and their objects and operations have changed with the change of the times, but many of them still bear in their charters and by-laws traces of the trade regulation which formed a great part of their original object.

The ordinances of the fraternity of Glovers of London, dated 1354, provided that no apprentice should be made a freeman at the end of his term without the consent of the Master and Wardens, and that no man of the craft should teach or inform a foreigner or stranger upon pain of 6*s.* 8*d.*, and generally that no man of the craft should disobey any rules lawfully made by the good advice of the Master and Wardens and other brethren of the craft.

The Blacksmiths of London made ordinances in 1434, that if any stranger came to London to have service in the craft, he shall be received in the craft to serve two weeks, and after that to make his covenant for three years, and to have for his salary 40*s*. a year, and shall do nothing pertaining to the craft without the counsel of the Warden; and that no servant of the craft shall sustain or succour a new man that cometh new to town to have service but in the form aforesaid.

The Shearmen or Cloth-workers in 1452 ordained that no man take an apprentice into the craft but he be free born and clean of body and of limbs, and not disfigured in any manner: and that if any man of the craft, or his apprentice, shear any cloth but it is truly wet he shall pay an arbitrary fine: and if any man take any chaffer of any Lombard or stranger, or receive any foreign man without license of the Wardens, he shall pay a fine.

These various rules were certified by the Commissary of the Bishop of London, with the view of making them binding upon the members, who could be sued in the Bishop's Court for breach of faith if they did not fulfil their undertaking to obey them. This ingenious method of using the ecclesiastical courts to enforce civil obligations was not looked upon with favour by the civil courts, and indeed had been prohibited in 1164, and again in 1220 and 1481. The judges were always hostile to agreements in restraint of trade. A case is in the law books for 1414, in which an action was brought against one John, a dyer, on a bond which he had given, undertaking not to use his craft of dyer for the space of half a year. Justice Hull said, the bond is void, for the condition of it is against the Common Law: and *per Dieu*, if the plaintiff were here, he should go to prison until he had paid a fine to the king.

It is possible that there are other instances where judges on the bench have been moved by righteous indignation beyond the verge of profanity; but it is doubtful whether there is another case in which the official reporter has felt bound to publish the fact. He usually takes the place of that recording angel whose compassionate tear expunged the oath into which Uncle Toby was surprised. Was there a reminiscence of this old case in the mind of Charles Dickens when he described the judge whose temper bordered on the irritable?

The legislature also sought, from very early times, to repress combinations of workmen. The long succession of acts for this purpose begins in 1304. In 1424 it was enacted that masons shall not confederate themselves in chapters and assemblies. Other acts having a similar object may be counted by the score. Side by side with them from the time of the plague of 1347 proceeded another series of acts, having the futile purpose of regulating wages by statute, instead of leaving them to be fixed by the operation of natural economic laws.

The trade guilds of London in due course obtained a legal constitution and exceptional privileges by Royal Charter. Each in respect of a particular trade acquired a control over the persons who should be allowed to practise it, and the manner in which it should be carried on; exercising that control partly for the benefit of the public, by seeing that the work put out came up to a certain standard of excellence, but mainly for that of the traders, by excluding the competition of foreigners, *i.e.* persons from other towns.

The modern Trade-union differs from these ancient combinations in many respects. Whether it is a union of employers or workmen, it is now mainly for the objects of regulating the relations of the one party with the other, and of imposing restrictions upon the conduct of the trade or business. The Trade-unions of workmen are the more common, but Trade-unions of employers are not unknown, and there are also Trade-unions which are, in effect, combinations against the consumer.

The old Combination Acts were repealed in 1824, and the act repealing them was itself repealed by an Act of 1825, which recited that combinations interfering with the free employment of capital and labour are injurious to trade and commerce, dangerous to the tranquillity of the country, and especially prejudicial to the interests of all who are concerned in them: and that it was expedient to make further provision, as well for the security and personal freedom of individual workmen in the disposal of their skill and labour, as for the security of the property and persons of masters and employers. It did not prohibit meetings of workmen for the sole purpose of consulting upon and determining the rate of wages to be required by the persons meeting, on the hours for which they will work: nor agreements entered into by workmen as to the same matters: nor meetings of masters for the sole purpose of consulting upon and determining the rate of wages to be paid by the persons meeting, or the hours of work to be required from those they employ: nor agreements entered into by masters as to the same matters.

By the Friendly Societies Act of 1855 provision was made that a society for any of the purposes of a Friendly Society, or for any purpose which was not illegal, might deposit its rules with the registrar, without fully registering them, and should thereupon have power to settle its own disputes, and to take proceedings against an officer, member, or person guilty of fraud or imposition, but should have no other privileges of the Act. This provision was resorted to by many Trade-unions, who relied on the declaration of the Act of 1825, that their purposes were not illegal, and desired to obtain protection for their funds: but the effect of it was much impaired by a series of legal decisions, which established that combinations in restraint of trade were illegal, and therefore that Trade-unions were not entitled to its benefits.

The earliest case arose in 1856, in respect of a combination of eighteen master cotton-spinners, who bound themselves under a penalty of £500 to act in compliance with the majority, in respect to carrying on or ceasing to carry on their works. The court held that a contract to carry on trade, not freely, as they ought to do, but in conformity to the will of others, was contrary to the public policy. A later case, in 1867, enlightened the Trade-unions of workmen as to the danger in which they were placed by the application of this doctrine. The president of the Bradford branch of the United Boiler-makers and Iron Ship-builders preferred a complaint against one of the officers, that he had unlawfully withheld money belonging to the society, and sought the remedy given by the Act of 1855.

The charge was proved; but the Justices dismissed the complaint on the ground that the society was for a purpose which was illegal. The Court of Queen's Bench confirmed the decision of the Justices, and held that where members agree not to work except on certain conditions, and the purpose of the Union is to support its members so out of employment in a manner consistent with the interests and wishes of the body, that was an illegal contract which could not be, and ought not to be, enforced.

Again, in 1869, the Amalgamated Society of Carpenters and Joiners sought to punish a fraudulent officer, but found themselves unable to do so, on the ground that the society had applied its funds to the support of workmen on strike, and to prevent men from seeking work in districts where a strike existed.

The result of these judgments was to place the funds of the Trade-unions at the mercy of their officials, and to give a distinct stimulus to fraud and dishonesty. The judges made themselves the accomplices and the protectors of the petty embezzler, and placed in his hands the disposal of those savings which represented so much heroic self-sacrifice on the part of the members. Fortunately, the legislature could be appealed to: and a short Act was passed in 1869 (drawn by Mr. J. M. Ludlow), providing that rules for determining the conditions on which members will or will not consent to employ or be employed, shall not, by reason only that such rules may operate in restraint of trade, be deemed, for the purpose of the punishment of frauds and impositions, to be rules for a purpose which is illegal.

At last, in 1871, the Trade-union Act was passed, which swept away all the antiquated theories of restraint of trade, and public policy, and the rest, and enacted that the purposes of any Trade-union shall not, by reason merely that they are in restraint of trade, be deemed to be unlawful, so as to render any member of such Trade-union liable to criminal prosecution for conspiracy or otherwise, or to be unlawful, so as to render void or voidable any agreement or trust. The least that can be said in favour of this statute is that it was a great discouragement to the rogues whom the legal decisions had encouraged. It was more; it was a full acknowledgment by the legislature of the right of working-men to combine together for their own benefit in their own way, and a substitution of lawful and ordered methods for methods of conflict with law.

By this Act, as amended in 1876, a Trade-union was defined to be any combination, whether temporary or permanent, for regulating the relations between workmen and masters, or between workmen and workmen, or between masters and masters, or for imposing restrictive conditions on the conduct of any trade or business, whether such combination would or would not before the passing of the Act have been deemed to have been an unlawful combination by reason of some one or more of its purposes being in restraint of trade. This Act authorized Trade-unions to be registered, and provided for registered Trade-unions a remedy against misapplication of funds and other privileges which were not extended to unregistered Trade-unions; but it was some years before several of the more important Trade-unions availed themselves of the advantages of registry. The proportion of unregistered Trade-unions is now comparatively small. Mr. and Mrs. Sidney Webb in their valuable history of Trade-unionism give a table which shows the membership of 28 unions, which had 343,890 members in 1890, as having risen to that number from 142,530 in 1870. In 1873, however, there were already 130 Trade-unions registered, and 93 of these had 256,179 members. There are now 565 registered Trade-unions in England and Wales.

The statistics of these Trade-unions (or rather of the 523 which on the 31st December, 1896, were of more than a full year's standing) throw some light on their method of working. At that day they had 1,036,351 members. Even from this figure something should be deducted for such Trade-unions as consist of employers only, and something also for cases where a branch of a Trade-union is separately registered, and its members are therefore counted twice over. These deductions are not very important, for the average number of members in an employers' trade-union is comparatively small, and the number of unregistered Trade-unions would largely exceed any that are counted twice. On the other hand, as the whole number of male adult workmen in the United Kingdom has been estimated by Sir Robert Giffen at 7,300,000, it is clear that the Trade-unions, registered and unregistered, comprise only a fractional part of the whole number of workmen.

The total income of these Trade-unions for the year 1896 was £1,693,150, or an average of £1, 12*s.* 8*d.* for every member, equivalent to a contribution of 7½*d.* per week. Of this, in the year, they only expended £1,258,440, increasing their funds by £434,710; so that at the end of the year those funds amounted to £2,138,296, or an average of £2, 1*s.* 3*d.* for each member. This is equivalent to a little more than fifteen months' income. Comparatively few of the Unions are of any magnitude. Out of the whole 523 there are only 22 which have more than 20,000 members, or more than £20,000 income, or more than £20,000 funds. Not one of these 22 had as much as four years' income accumulated; eight of them had less than one year's income in hand. This is a point of which we shall presently see the importance.

The Trade-union which was, at the date in question, by far the largest and most important of all was the

Amalgamated Society of Engineers, a society which was established in 1851. It did not take advantage of the permission to register given by the Act of 1871 until 1884. As it was engaged during 1897 in a long and exhausting struggle with the employers in the engineering trade, it will be interesting to trace by its proceedings during 1896 to what extent it had become prepared for such a struggle. During the year 1896 the Amalgamated Society of Engineers increased its members from 79,134 to 87,313, its income from £296,960 to £347,867, and its funds from £206,116 to £305,882. Its income was therefore nearly £4 per member, or one shilling and sixpence per member per week, and it saved out of that income enough to increase its funds by £99,766, though the funds even then were less than one year's income. In 1897 the great lock-out took place; the members raised in contributions £441,940; the public subscribed £77,765; other Trade-unions lent £22,900; and the Union was able not only to keep up its payments for death, accident, sickness, and superannuation, amounting to £126,694, but to grant trade benefits amounting to £527,010. At the end of the year it had in its general fund £93,255, and in its superannuation fund (which had been kept intact) £63,597. The number of members had increased to 91,444.

The oldest existing registered Trade-union is the London Society of Compositors, which was established in 1785. It had at the end of 1896 10,558 members, £32,008 income, and £44,645 funds, having increased its funds during the year by £12,211. It appears from Johnson's *Typographia* that in the year 1785 a regular scale of compositors' wages was for the first time printed, and was agreed to by a general meeting of the master printers. There had been, however, almost from the introduction of printing, a system of internal regulation in a printing-office, called the "chapel". When a printer had a complaint to make against a comrade, he would tell it to the president or "father" of the chapel, who would call a chapel at the imposing-stone, and determine the matter in dispute, and amerce the plaintiff or defendant, according as the charge was proved or rebutted.

The Manchester Society of Braziers and Sheet-metal Workers dates back to the year 1802, but was not registered until 1890. It is a comparatively small union, having only 523 members, an income of £1781, and £1419 funds, having increased its funds during the year from £838. This tends to show that great fluctuations in the funds of a Trade-union do not affect its continued existence.

Another old Trade-union is the Friendly Society of Ironfounders of England, Ireland, and Wales, established in 1809. It has 16,278 members, £61,085 income, and £46,341 funds, having shared the general forward movement of the year by an increase of £20,088 in its funds. This society has an interesting history, and has taken a creditable part in movements for the benefit of the workmen belonging to it.

That workmen should have achieved such results as these in the face of the bitter persecution that was directed against combinations of working-men in the early part of this century, and of the cruel punishment inflicted upon some of their members for an imaginary offence—despite also their own mistakes and the real crimes which were committed by some trade organizations in Sheffield and elsewhere—is evidence of the vitality of workmen's trade combinations, and of their necessity in the circumstances of modern life.

The registered Trade-unions in Scotland and Ireland should not be passed over. In Scotland, 36 unions had 62,634 members, and an income of £80,505. Their funds on 31st December, 1896, amounted to £95,586, having increased in the year from £77,232. Only one society, the Associated Ironmoulders of Scotland (akin to the Ironfounders in England) ranks with the 22 largest English unions. In Ireland also 36 unions made returns, but their operations are very small, and the whole of them put together would not rank with the 22 large unions in England. They had an aggregate of 7522 members, £14,504 income, and £14,139 funds, an increase during the year from £11,903. The oldest is the Belfast Brassfounders, established in 1840, having 177 members and £458 funds.

In the year 1872 a Trade-union was established among the agricultural labourers, a class which had been reduced to a miserable condition of poverty. A previous Union of Agricultural Labourers in Dorsetshire in 1834 had been suppressed by the infliction on six of its members of the ferocious sentence of seven years' transportation. Mr. Joseph Arch, the founder of the new union, had not the same fate to fear, but he did experience bitter and unscrupulous opposition. The Union succeeded in bettering the condition of the agricultural labourer, and contributed to obtain for him the parliamentary franchise; after a stormy experience of twenty years it completed its circle of usefulness and ceased to exist.

In order that a Trade-union may be registered, it has to adopt rules providing for the following matters:—

1. The name of the Trade-union, which must not be the same as that of any existing registered Trade-

union, nor so nearly resemble such name as to be likely to deceive the members or the public. It has been held also that rules under the name of an existing unregistered Trade-union cannot be registered unless it is shown that the applicants for registry are authorized on its behalf.

2. The place of meeting for its business, which may or may not be the same as its registered office. When the registered office is changed, notice is to be given to the Registrar.
3. The whole of the objects for which it is to be established.
4. The purposes for which the funds thereof shall be applicable. If any of such purposes shall be unlawful, the registration is void, and may be cancelled.
5. The conditions under which any member may become entitled to any benefits assured.
6. The fines and forfeitures to be imposed on any member. These must be definite.
7. The manner of making, altering, amending, and rescinding rules.
8. The appointment and removal of

   (*a*) A general committee of management,
   (*b*) A trustee or trustees,
   (*c*) Treasurer,
   (*d*) Other officers.

9. The investment of the funds.
10. An annual or periodical audit of accounts.
11. The inspection of the books and names of the members by every person having an interest in the funds.
12. The manner of dissolving the Trade-union.

If the Rules contain these provisions, and do not disclose an unlawful purpose, they are to be registered. It is not necessary for the Registrar to inquire what other provisions the rules contain.

The primary and paramount object of a Trade-union is its trade object:—if it be a workmen's union, the so using their funds that they can, in case of need, resist any attempt of the employers to lower the scale of wages, or to render the conditions of labour more severe, or enforce any attempt of the workmen to raise the scale of wages, or to render the conditions of labour more lenient; if it be an employers' union, the converse. Workmen's unions, especially those of the older type, combine with this object, very greatly to the advantage of the members, other purposes, akin to those of a friendly society, such as relief in sickness, pensions in old age, allowances when out of work, assistance towards emigration, and provision for funeral expenses at death.

In ordinary times, when no trade conflict exists, the expenditure on these purposes largely exceeds the expenditure on trade purposes. For example, in the year 1890, when the total expenditure of 259 trade-unions, registered and unregistered, as recorded by Mr. Burnett, the able Chief Labour Correspondent of the Board of Trade, was £862,000 (the number of members being 871,000), only £107,000 was spent in dispute benefits. Of the remainder £173,000 was for sick pay and medical attendance, £145,000 for out-of-work benefits, £87,000 for superannuation, £60,000 for funerals, and £26,000 for accident and other benefits. Sick pay, superannuation and funeral allowance are benefits which can only be secured (as we shall see when we discuss Friendly Societies) by the accumulation of considerable funds to meet the future accruing liabilities, and those funds should be earmarked for each benefit and set aside, so that as the age of the members increases, and the liability to sickness becomes more urgent, and old age draws nearer, and deaths are more numerous, the funds may be ready to meet the growing claims. This is the moral every actuary is constantly preaching.

The members of Trade-unions, knowing what they want, disregard the teaching of the actuary. They do not accumulate large funds, and do not earmark those funds for a special purpose, with an exception to be mentioned hereafter. There is not a single large Trade-union, as we have seen, which has as much as four years' income in hand, and the average of all the unions is fifteen months' income only. The common practice is to levy each year as much as is required to meet the outgoings of the year, and only to keep in hand a little over one year's income, except when the probability of a conflict is in the air, and it becomes necessary to increase the contributions of the members and accumulate a reserve to support them when the conflict comes. It is always to be remembered that the paramount purpose of the Trade-union is the trade purpose.

The actuaries would point out, very justly, that to raise the sick pay, and superannuation allowances, and funeral money, which all increase as the age of the member increases, and in the case of superannuation allowances are deferred for many years, by an equal levy on all members alike, is a practice which is unjust to the younger men and unduly favourable to the older men. If younger men were practically free to join or not to join the union, and if they understood their own interests, they would not join a body in which funds for those benefits were raised by levy; and in that event the old men would be left to themselves, and the levy would year by year have to be greater, till at last it would be more than they could pay. It is because they know that the trade purposes are those to which, in case of need, all the others must give way, that it becomes the interest of the younger men to support the union.

It is essential, therefore, that a Trade-union supported by levy should have the means of practically ensuring that as young men entered the trade they should have no option of refusing to join the union and to contribute to its funds a levy of the same amount as that paid by the older men, who would nevertheless derive a much larger share of the benefit of the levy. It is also essential, especially having regard to the long-deferred benefit of superannuation allowance, that a Trade-union which relies upon levies should be connected with a progressive industry—that is to say, that its members should increase from time to time, and not remain stationary or diminish, if it is to meet the growing burden of the allowances.

Of the younger men who join a union, about half will live to be of the pension age. By the system of levy, the present members have to pay the pensions of those who were young forty or fifty years ago. If there are now 5000 members, and there were only 500 then, the burden might not be intolerable, because it would be measured by the claims of the survivors of the 500. If, however, we look forward another forty or fifty years, and the Trade-union should not increase its members beyond its present number of 5000, or, worse still, should diminish them, the burden would probably become intolerable, because it would be measured by the claims of the survivors of the 5000, a large proportion of whom are now comparatively young. This consideration has impressed itself upon the minds of some of the more thoughtful among the members of Trade-unions, who have commenced to set aside a special fund to meet superannuation allowance. As yet, however, this special fund has not been sufficiently long in operation to form an adequate provision, and it is only to be noted as a step in the right direction. The special fund of the Engineers, for example, which was not touched during the recent strike, does not yet amount to one year's pension.

One advantage that has always been held to attach to the system of an equal undivided levy for all benefits is that it tends to caution in entering upon industrial warfare, and therefore to the prevention of strikes for any cause short of necessity, the members knowing that the cost of the strike must diminish the funds applicable for other benefits. The result has been that these Trade-unions have been in many cases organizations by which the claims of the workmen have been secured by friendly negotiations with the employers, who have found it advantageous to deal with an organized body representing the workmen, and consisting of the best informed and most reasonable among their number, disposed rather to avoid than to incur hostile proceedings.

The success which attended the strike of the dock workers, organized by the Dock Workers' Union in 1889, led to the creation of a large number of Trade-unions on a different principle, mainly among unskilled labourers. The new unionism, as it was called, disparaged the system of insurance for provident purposes, and adopted instead the purely militant trade organization. Of 500 Trade-unions registered between 1888 and 1895, 200 have already ceased to exist. This and other circumstances lead to the opinion that the combined form of trade-union is the more advantageous to the members, notwithstanding the unscientific and uncertain conditions under which its benefits are offered.

It is but justice to the Trade-unions to add, that their members have made great sacrifices in order to keep faith with those to whom superannuation and other allowances have been promised. The statute strangely provides that nothing it contains shall enable any court to entertain any legal proceeding instituted with the object of directly enforcing or recovering damages for the breach of any agreement for the application of the funds of a Trade-union to provide benefits to members. It is creditable to the Trade-unions that, being thus left to be a law to themselves, and the members deprived of legal remedy if the Trade-union refuses to grant the benefits it has agreed to provide, there should be few, if any, complaints of unjust treatment raised against them.

In a separate report made by the Duke of Devonshire and other members of the Royal Commission on Labour, this matter was considered, and a recommendation was made that an option should be given to Trade-unions of obtaining incorporation, and thus becoming bodies capable of suing and being sued, and that in respect of such incorporated Trade-unions the section in question should not apply. The recommendation has not been acted upon, and was not received by the Trade-unions with favour. They have a strong sentiment against having recourse to courts of law, and in favour of their own method of settling their disputes; and it is not perhaps surprising that that sentiment should still exist, though many years have elapsed since the decisions of which they complained.

Those years have witnessed a large extension in the influence and power of Trade-unions. They have gained a considerable representation in Parliament, and the views of their members are consulted by both the great political parties. Although the Trade-unions do not comprise more than one-fourth, or perhaps even one-fifth, of the working-men of the country, they are taken as expressing the general views of the whole body. They have been fortunate in the personal character of some of their representatives. Mr. George Howell, the author of *Conflicts of Capital and Labour*, *Trade-unionism New and Old*, a *Handy Book of the Labour Laws*, and other works, during a long parliamentary career acquired the esteem of all parties, and succeeded in passing many measures for the benefit of the working-classes. Others, such as Mr. Macdonald, Mr. Broadhurst, Mr. Cremer, may be mentioned in the same connection. The unions have not only directly obtained benefits for their members, but they have acted indirectly as educational institutions, and have opened a career of public service to many among their number who have shown themselves capable of attaining distinction.

The generous manner in which the various trades contribute to the support of each other in times of stress is a further indication of the excellent moral influence exerted by those "combinations of workmen" which the legislature used to brand as criminal.

Chapter III.

Friendly Societies.

The theoretical young workman, whose existence we conjectured at the beginning of the last chapter, may belong to a trade which is not organized, or he may not think it worth while to join the union which is connected with his trade, or he may recognize the fact that, from its peculiar constitution, a Trade-union is not the best form of provision for provident purposes other than trade purposes. In any of these cases he will find in the Friendly Society a provision which he wants and cannot afford to neglect. We shall accordingly now proceed to consider what a Friendly Society is, and to look into the methods adopted by the various classes of friendly societies, and the nature of the benefits which they confer on the persons who join them.

The legal definition of a Friendly Society is a society for the purpose of providing by voluntary subscriptions of the members thereof, with or without the aid of donations, for

(*a*) The relief or maintenance of the members, their husbands, wives, children, fathers, mothers, brothers or sisters, nephews or nieces, or wards being orphans, during sickness or other infirmity, whether bodily or mental, in old age (which means any age after 50) or in widowhood, or for the relief or maintenance of the orphan children of members during minority: or

(*b*) Insuring money to be paid on the death of a member's child or on the death of a member, or for the funeral expenses of the husband, wife, or child of a member, or of the widow of a deceased member, or, as regards persons of the Jewish persuasion, for the payment of a sum of money during the period of confined mourning: or

(*c*) The relief or maintenance of the members when on travel in search of employment, or when in distressed circumstances, or in case of shipwreck or loss or damage of or to boats or nets: or

(*d*) The endowment of members or nominees of members at any age: or

(*e*) The assurance against loss by fire, to any amount not exceeding £15, of the tools or implements of the trade or calling of the members.

Few societies combine the whole of these objects: the majority insuring only sick pay and a sum at death.

In order that the privileges conceded to societies registered under the Friendly Societies Act may not be abused by their extension to persons of ample means, it is provided that no gross sum shall be insured exceeding £200 and no annuity exceeding £50, and in regard to the privilege of exemption from income-tax, that it shall not apply to a society that assures annuities exceeding £30.

Friendly Societies can claim an even greater antiquity than Trade-unions. In their earliest form they were burial societies. It is a very common weakness of human nature to surround the disposal of a dead body with circumstances of pomp and expenditure which exceed anything the deceased enjoyed when living, and tax heavily the means of the survivors. When religion began to be organized, its policy was to avail itself of this instinctive tendency of mankind, and to encourage rather than to discourage the desire to bestow costly observances upon the deceased. The idea of a spirit, separable from the body, and capable of being benefited by these attentions, arose, and a professional caste for conducting the ceremonies was set apart.

Examples of this sentiment are to be found in the ancient interments, in which objects supposed to be useful to the deceased in his future state, the coin he was to pay to Charon, food and personal ornaments, favourite horses and other animals, were buried with him—leading even to the fanaticism of his favourite wives destroying themselves that he might still enjoy the society that gave him pleasure in life. This tendency of mankind to give up precious things for the benefit of the departed, modified by religious systems into the purchase of masses, and degenerating into various forms of ostentation and pretence, led to the survivors impoverishing themselves, and to their making appeals for help to their neighbours and comrades, especially where they came together in social meetings.

It was not a long or difficult step to reduce this casual help to an organized tariff, and to raise the funds payable for funeral expenses by an equal levy on all the members of the social gathering; and the next step, of establishing a permanent chaplain who should pray for the souls of all the deceased members, almost naturally followed. It appears that in China there have been for many centuries burial clubs, termed long-life loan companies, and that they exist in almost all the towns and villages. There are also traces of similar clubs in Greek and Roman epigraphy, and the Teutonic gild is familiar to all of us. As there is here no question of intercommunication, we see in this class of society a sort of spontaneous growth.

The rules of a Roman burial club of the time of Hadrian, founded at Lanuvium, and dedicated to Antinous and Diana, have come down to our own times.

The members met once a month, and frequently dined together. They excluded a member from benefit who did not keep up his subscription; but when a member died who was not in arrear, they followed his body in a walking procession and paid the expenses of the funeral. If it took place at too great a distance for their personal attendance, they refunded the expenses to the person who had charitably defrayed them. Nothing was to be done, however, in regard to the funeral of a member who committed suicide—a curious exception when it is remembered that to commit suicide is to seek death *Romano more*. Opprobrious or contumelious speech to the master was punishable by a fine, and it was his duty upon certain appointed days to perform solemn offices in white vestments. Whether our own mediæval guilds (to the trade-unionist aspect of which we have already referred in Chapter II.) were the lineal descendants of these or of the Teutonic gilds does not much matter. At least one Roman club, the college of the smiths, is known to have existed during the Roman occupation of this country; and the late Mr. Coote has shown conclusively how much that was Roman survived that occupation.

The late Mr. Cornelius Walford compiled from the rules of the mediæval guilds the following list of their provident objects:—

1. Relief in poverty.
2. Relief in sickness.
3. Relief in old age.
4. Relief on loss of sight.
5. Relief on loss of limb.
6. Relief on loss of cattle.
7. Relief on fall of a house

8. Relief on making pilgrimages.
9. Relief in case of loss by fire.
10. Relief in case of loss by floods.
11. Relief in case of loss by robbery.
12. Relief in case of loss by shipwreck.
13. Relief in case of imprisonment.
14. Relief for defence at law.
15. Relief of the deaf and dumb.
16. Relief of the afflicted with leprosy.
17. Dowries on marriage of females, or on their entering a house of religion.
18. Aid in temporary pecuniary difficulties.
19. Aid to obtain work.
20. Repair of roads and bridges.

The list is even more comprehensive than that in the Friendly Societies Act 1896, which we have quoted already, and seems to include every possible ill that man is heir to; especially when it is remembered that these provident purposes were largely supplemented by works of charity.

The evidence of any direct connection between the guilds of the middle ages and the modern Friendly Society is scanty, if indeed there can be said to be any such evidence at all. The oldest existing societies, founded in 1687, 1703, and 1708, are those which were founded among the Huguenot refugee workmen in Spitalfields, and the modern London Friendly Society is one of the boons those admirable men conferred upon this country in return for its hospitality. Friendly Societies first appeared upon the statute-book in the year 1793, when an Act was passed for their encouragement and relief. The preamble of that Act affirmed that the protection and encouragement of such societies would be likely to be attended with very beneficial effects by promoting the happiness of individuals and at the same time diminishing the public burdens.

The public burden which the framer of the statute had in mind was no doubt that of poor-law relief: and one of the privileges the statute extended to members of Friendly Societies was that of exemption from removal under the poor-law until they became actually chargeable to the parish. Having regard to the vicious principles upon which poor-law relief was then administered, there is something to be said for the view that Friendly Societies greatly diminished the burden upon the public. The same argument is still used, but it is submitted that it has ceased to have the same weight. Since the great reform of the poor-law that took place in 1834, it has been applied with more or less strictness to its proper purpose of the relief of destitution. That reform has undoubtedly led to the formation of Friendly Societies, but it is another thing to say that the societies have saved so much in poor-rates. That would be to imply that their members, if they had not belonged to such societies, would have been destitute. Whether they would have been so or not, no one can tell. We think it is a libel upon them to say that they would. If they had not invested their savings in Friendly Societies, they would presumably have invested them elsewhere. A Friendly Society creates no wealth. It only husbands and distributes it.

The Friendly Society has done so much for its members, and contributed so largely to industrial welfare by increasing their self-respect and independence,—it has been so powerful an instrument of foresight and economy, and has led so many men to positions of influence and of dignity,—that it has strong and genuine claims upon the community, whose interests it has largely promoted. It is precisely for that reason that we do not wish to see urged on its behalf a claim that cannot be substantiated, and that from our point of view implies a disparagement of the member of a Friendly Society that he does not deserve, for there is no evidence whatever that the class of men from whom the members of Friendly Societies are drawn is the class of men who would otherwise be paupers. Such evidence as there is is all to the contrary. The late Mr. Ballan Stead, secretary of the Ancient Order of Foresters, stated in his testimony before the Royal Commission on the Aged Poor that out of the half-million of members who constituted that society, he could not find that there were as many as a hundred persons in receipt of relief under the poor-law. This is the more remarkable that the society itself does not insure (in the generality of cases) relief in old age as such, but only grants a sick allowance to an aged member when he is suffering from some defined disease which disables him from work, and even then the allowance, after short terms of full- and half-pay, is reduced to quarter-pay of *2s. 6d.* or *3s.* a week. As the society does not directly insure him against pauperism in old age, we have to seek in some other direction for an explanation of the reason for his not becoming a pauper, and we find it in the moral character of the man himself. The considerations which induce him to belong to a Friendly Society are the same considerations which keep him independent of public aid in his old age.

The existing law of Friendly Societies is consolidated in the Friendly Societies Act 1896, and the Collecting Societies and Industrial Assurance Companies Act 1896. By registry under the Friendly Societies Act a society becomes entitled to certain privileges. The condition of registry is the adopting rules which contain provisions for the following matters:—

1. The name of the society, which must not be a name identical with that of any existing registered society, or so nearly resemble any such name as to deceive, nor must it be any name likely to deceive the members or the public as to the nature or identity of the society.
2. The place of office. Any change in the society's office must be notified to the registrar within fourteen days, so that the public may at all times know where a society is to be found.
3. The whole of the objects for which the society is to be established, which must be some of those specified in the act as above set forth.
4. The purposes for which the funds thereof shall be applicable, which must be such as are requisite for carrying out those objects.
5. The terms of admission of members.
6. The conditions under which any member may become entitled to any benefit assured, so that there may be no doubt as to a member's right to benefit.
7. The fines and forfeitures to be imposed on any member, which must be definite and not arbitrary.
8. The consequences of non-payment of any subscription or fine. As the subscriptions are voluntary, the consequences of non-payment can only be the loss of benefit or exclusion from the society.
9. The mode of holding meetings.
10. The right of voting, which may be restricted to certain classes of the members.
11. The manner of making, altering, or rescinding rules.

12. The appointment and removal of a committee of management, to whom may be assigned any name, such as "directors", the society thinks fit.
13. The appointment and removal of a treasurer and other officers. The treasurer must be an individual, not a corporation.
14. The appointment and removal of trustees. The committee, treasurer, and trustees must all be over 21 years of age.
15. When the society is one having branches, provision is to be made also for

    (*a*) The composition of the central body;
    (*b*) The conditions under which a branch may secede from the society.

    The central fund of the society, and the separate fund of each branch, should also be defined in the rules.
16. The investment of the funds. A society may invest its funds on any security expressly directed by its rules, but not on any security not so directed, except by way of a deposit in a savings-bank or with the Commissioners for the Reduction of the National Debt. The rules may not direct any investment upon personal security, except by way of a loan on the society's own policies, or a loan from a separate loan fund.
17. The keeping of the accounts.
18. Audit once a year at least. This may be conducted either by two persons appointed by the society or by one of the public auditors appointed by the Treasury, if the society prefer to employ him. It is not compulsory to do so.
19. Annual returns to the registrar of the receipts.

funds, effects, expenditure, and number of members of the society. These are to be made by the 1st June in each year.

20. The inspection of the books of the society by every person having an interest in its funds. This is to be permitted at all reasonable hours at the registered office of the society or at any place where the books are kept. Where the society grants loans to members, the loan account of a member is not to be inspected by another member without his consent.

21. The manner in which disputes shall be settled. As to this the society is perfectly free to adopt any manner of settlement it thinks fit, except that the committee of management, being necessary parties to the dispute, cannot be judges in their own cause.

22. Where the society divides its funds, it must make provision for meeting all claims existing upon the society at the time of division before the division takes place.

23. Keeping separate accounts of all money received or paid on account of every particular fund or benefit assured for which a separate table of contributions payable is adopted.

24. Keeping a separate account of the expenses of management and of all contributions on account thereof.

25. A valuation once in every five years of the assets and liabilities of the society, including the estimated risks and contributions.

26. The voluntary dissolution of the society by the consent of five-sixths in value of its members (a certain increase of voting value being given to the

older members) and of all those entitled to the actual receipt of benefit at the time.

27. The right of a specified proportion of the members to apply to the Chief Registrar for an investigation of the affairs of the society or for winding it up.

It results necessarily that the rules of each society form a comprehensive code, in which the members are fully informed of the conditions of their contract with each other, and of the remedies which the law provides to secure its due fulfilment, and to enable the individual member to obtain his rights, to watch over the proceedings of the managing body of the society, and to check mismanagement or fraud. The registry office has prepared model rules, which are printed on sheets of foolscap, on one side only; so that the persons intending to form a Friendly Society need only add to the model rules the details of their own particular plan, and send the rules thus framed to the registrar for revision. Otherwise, it is possible they might feel some alarm at the long list of matters they are required to provide for.

There are some points which it is interesting to note in respect of this code of requirements. The first is, that although the society is required to state what are the conditions under which its benefits are to be insured, no conditions are imposed upon it: its members are perfectly free to insert in the rules any conditions they may think fit. They may promise themselves large benefits for small contributions, if they care to do so. They are not under any compulsion to adopt graduated rates of contribution, or to consult an actuary as to what rates they can charge with safety for sick pay or funeral allowance: they may provide for a periodical distribution of their funds, provided only that they meet such claims as are actually incumbent upon them at the time of the distribution: they are left entirely to their own discretion as to the soundness of the conditions on which they grant insurances.

The legislature leaves the societies equally free to manage their affairs in their own way. The registrar has no authority to interfere unless the members themselves call upon him to do so. Even then, he has no power to impose upon the society his own views as to any reforms that may appear to him necessary. The society works out its own salvation. It is true that every society has once in every five years to employ a valuer to value its assets and liabilities. It may employ as such valuer any person who is willing to undertake the work, and when the valuation is made, it is under no obligation to take any action upon it, or to adopt any advice the valuer may give. It may go on its own way to the bitter end.

From first to last, therefore, the essential principle of the Friendly Societies Act is the voluntary principle. The act compels no society to be registered; it compels no registered society to adopt any fixed scale of contributions and benefits; it compels no society to carry on its business in any particular way; it compels no society to adopt reforms, however apparent may be the necessity. What the act does provide, however, is that the members of a society shall have ample means of knowing what are the contracts into which they are entering, how their managers are carrying on the business, what is the financial condition of the concern, and of themselves originating and carrying into effect the reforms which the periodical valuations from time to time show to be necessary.

Though under the act registry is optional, yet as

organization and management are voluntary, and the act attaches a number of privileges to registry, which, in the aggregate, are valuable, it would seem surprising that any society should reject these privileges: nevertheless, it is the fact that for one reason or another a vast number of societies—occupying probably as large a field as that occupied by the registered societies—remain unregistered. The advantages which a registered society has over an unregistered society are the following:—

1. It can legally hold land and other kinds of property in the names of the trustees.
2. When the property is copyhold land, it may require that three trustees should be admitted on payment of the same fines and fees as a single tenant.
3. Where the property is stock in the funds, it may be transferred from a deceased or absent trustee by order of the Chief Registrar, without other legal proceedings.
4. All other property, including land that is not copyhold, passes from one trustee to another without conveyance or assignment.
5. Its trustees can carry on all legal proceedings on its behalf.
6. They can invest its money with the National Debt Commissioners at a fixed rate of interest, and thus be independent of the rise and fall of stock.
7. They can invest its money without restriction of amount in a Savings-bank or Post-office Savings-bank.
8. They can discharge a mortgage on which money of the society has been invested by merely endorsing a receipt upon it, without a reconveyance.
9. They can take proceedings against an officer for mis-

application of funds, although such misapplication does not amount to larceny or embezzlement.

10. Where they do not take such proceedings, the Registrar, or the Committee of Management, may take them, or may authorize a member to do so.
11. The trustees are entitled to claim property of the society from the representatives of a deceased or bankrupt member in preference to all other creditors, and even to claim priority over an execution creditor.
12. They, or the committee, or a general meeting, can call upon officers to render an account and to deliver up property in their possession.
13. Documents of the society are exempt from stamp-duty.
14. Certificates of birth or death of members, or persons insured, can be obtained at a reduced fee.
15. Members may be admitted at any age exceeding one year, and when over sixteen by themselves, or under sixteen by their parents and guardians, may execute instruments and give discharges.
16. Members may insure the funeral expenses of their wives and children without risk of forfeiture for want of insurable interest.
17. Members above sixteen years of age may dispose of sums not exceeding £100, payable at their death, by a written nomination.
18. The trustees, where a member dies intestate and has made no nomination, may pay to the person who appears to them to be legally entitled, and such payment is a good discharge to the society.
19. They may pay on the death of a person of illegitimate birth as if he had been legitimate.
20. They can settle disputes in any manner the rules provide, and thus avoid the cost of litigation.

21. Societies are entitled to the services of public auditors and public valuers at moderate fixed charges.
22. Societies (if they grant no annuities exceeding £30) are free of income-tax either under Schedule C or Schedule D.
23. Their rules, removals, appointments of trustees, returns, and valuations, are placed on record at a public office, where they can be inspected.
24. Copies and extracts of all registered documents attested by the registrar are receivable in evidence in courts of justice.

Some of these privileges—such as the exemption from stamp-duty and from income-tax, and the profit rates of interest on investments with the National Debt Commissioners—are actual endowments by the State; others enable the society to do inexpensively that which other citizens can only do at heavy cost; and others are of great value for the protection of the funds and the due carrying into effect the objects of the society.

According to the latest complete return of registered societies published, 22,313 Friendly Societies and branches in England and Wales had 3,861,519 members and £21,410,563 funds. In Scotland, 1325 societies and branches had 283,512 members and £1,218,090 funds. In Ireland, 360 societies and branches had 58,570 members and £66,386 funds. The total for the United Kingdom was 23,998 societies and branches, having 4,203,601 members and £22,695,039 funds.

In addition, there were Collecting Burial Societies, which are registered under "The Friendly Societies Act", but are subject to special regulations under "The Collecting Societies Act 1896", and whose members include a large number of children. Of these, 35 in England and Wales had 3,318,942 members and £2,289,858 funds; and eight in Scotland had 556,273 members and £423,356 funds. The total for the United Kingdom (there being none in Ireland) was 43 societies with 3,875,215 members and £2,713,214 funds. The difference between the two classes of societies is marked by the fact that in the ordinary Friendly Society the funds are £5, 8*s*. per member; in the Collecting Burial Society only 14*s*. per member.

The total for the United Kingdom of the two classes of societies together was 24,041 societies and branches, having 8,078,816 members and £25,408,253 funds.

Chapter IV.

Varieties of Friendly Society.

Our hypothetical young man will find himself called upon to select the particular society he will join. One consequence of the absolute freedom and voluntariness, which has been shown to be the leading characteristic of the law relating to Friendly Societies, is that each society has been at liberty to organize itself in any manner which has appeared to the members to be most suitable to their circumstances. We have accordingly a great variety of societies. The Royal Commission on Friendly Societies enumerated as many as seventeen classes. It would be outside the scope of this work to express a preference for one class over another, or to recommend one class at the cost of the others, but we may proceed to describe the various methods of management, so as to give the reader the means of exercising a judgment of his own.

The oldest and most simple form—the one that shows most traces of continuity with the ancient guilds—is the village club. Meeting for the most part at the village inn—having its box for donations by way of casual relief, and its box with three locks for the securities, documents, and uninvested cash, its solemn procession to church on the anniversary day—often a day selected from some association with local history—it is largely a relic of the olden time. Its organization is usually very simple. It too often has a uniform contribution for all ages at entry, to assure sick pay during life and burial money at death. Its funds keep on increasing while its members are young till it gets a tidy little sum, which it probably invests on a mortgage of a bit of property. When its members grow old, the claims for sick pay increase, and the funds begin to diminish, till at last they diminish so rapidly that the old men share out what there is and close the society. The young men have long since learned that there is no advantage to them in joining the society merely for the purpose of paying sick pay to the older men, but they have not learned much more wisdom: they start another club for themselves on the same principle, think all is going well as long as the funds continue to increase, and then in their turn grow old; and so the vicious succession is kept up, each club in its turn lasting out its one generation of members.

Some village clubs have seen the mischief of these old methods, have adopted graduated scales of contribution and other sound principles, and have met with proportionate success. The circumstance that such clubs can rarely have a large average of members is against them, but there is great compensation in the consideration that the members generally will be well acquainted with each other. Early in the century the Rev. J. T. Becher, prebendary of Southwell, devised a plan for village societies, and several were founded on his system. They were a great improvement on the old-fashioned clubs, but have now for the most part terminated. One of the latest survivors is the Stewponey Becher Club, in a locality that Mr. Baring Gould has lately made famous.

As the Orders of Oddfellows, Shepherds, Druids, Foresters, and the like, grew in popularity, the type of the village club was transformed into the type of the lodge, and in the early days of those orders their lodges or other divisions presented the same features of disregard of science in equal contributions for all ages and otherwise that we have seen in the village club, and were exposed to the same consequences. In speaking of the early days of those Orders, we are not alluding to their claims of misty antiquity, as having been first established among the Roman soldiers in the time of the Emperor Nero and the like, but rather to the time when they began to be active in the various towns and villages of the country, and to establish themselves as bodies with definite friendly-society benefits.

With Mr. Frome Wilkinson, we believe that the oldest of the Orders did not originate earlier than the first half of the eighteenth century, and that they had much to do with the revival of Freemasonry during that period. He quotes the Order of Free Gardeners in Scotland, established in 1715, as the earliest that can now be traced. Like Freemasonry, they were at first mainly convivial, incidentally charitable, and not provident. The late editor of the *Oddfellows' Magazine* holds that while the Masonic Order maintained intact the traditions of the

Masons' craft guild, the Oddfellows comprised a collection from all the others, which were not strong enough in themselves to carry on a distinctive club. Thus they were not mercers, nor dyers, nor smiths, nor girdlers, nor drapers, but an *omnium gatherum*, and hence "Oddfellows". The similarity of ritual and ceremonial is thus fully accounted for.

If the Oddfellows had followed the same course as the Freemasons, and secured as members "noblemen and gentlemen of the first rank", they would probably have become the same harmless, semi-convivial, semi-benevolent body that the Freemasons, in this country at least, now are. It is fortunate for them that they remained a society of "good-fellowship", consisting of members of the same rank of life, and asking for no patronage. The way was thus left open for their evolution into a great Friendly Society. They began with convivial objects, and with a casual method of relief to distressed brothers. They found that, to prevent abuse, and to save the self-respect of such members as might fall into distress, it would be better to raise the fund by a fixed contribution, and to give the member a definite claim to benefit.

The allowance during sickness, however, continued to bear, in the familiar expression "sick gift", testimony to the original voluntary nature of the relief, as Mr. Moffrey points out, just as the word "donation" is generally used by Trade-unions to denote the sums allowed to members on strike. To Trade-unions the term is the more applicable, as there is no legal right to sue for the benefits; but to the assurance of sick pay by friendly societies it is not now applicable at all. A further development of the system arose when it was found that the provision of burial money by the lodge would sometimes, when several deaths had occurred, involve a very heavy payment, while at other times years might pass without any payment whatever. The plan of equalizing such payments by combining the lodges, as far as burial money was concerned, into "districts" at once put an end to this fluctuation, and prepared the way for complete organization of the orders. The society so organized is popularly, if not quite accurately, called an "affiliated Order". Its designation under the statute is "a society having branches". Such societies were not admitted to registry until 1850, and the Act of 1855, which admitted their branches to registry, did so under the perplexing condition that each branch was to be registered as a separate society.

The Act of 1875, introduced and carried through by Sir Stafford Northcote, Chancellor of the Exchequer, afterwards Earl of Iddesleigh, for the first time gave full recognition to the constitution which such societies had worked out for themselves, and by so doing greatly strengthened the bond between the central body of a society and its local branches, and furthered the judicious measures by which several of the Orders have been enabled materially to improve the condition of their branches. Sir Stafford Northcote, in his capacity of chairman of the Royal Commission on Friendly Societies, had thoroughly acquainted himself with, and learned to appreciate, the work of the Orders, and the statute bears the impress of the sound sense and considerateness that were marked features of his character.

In every Society having branches, it is necessary that there should be:—

1. A central body, of such composition as the rules of the Society direct.

2. A fund under the control of the central body, to which each branch is bound to contribute.
3. A fund administered by each branch, or by a committee or officers appointed by the branch.
4. A declaration in the rules, of what control the central body shall have over each branch.
5. Provision enabling the branch to secede from the Society.

A branch cannot alter its rules, or obtain an official inspection, or apply to the Chief Registrar to call a special meeting, or for an award of dissolution, or dissolve itself, without the consent of the central body.

In the constitution which the legislature has thus impressed upon these Societies, there is a mixture of centralization with local independence that is very valuable. The administration of the local fund—which is in general the fund for sickness—is expressly reserved to the branch, which in other respects is under the control of the central body, subject to the rules.

The supreme government of each order is vested in an annual or other periodical general meeting, composed of delegates elected by the several branches. This meeting, in a large Order, extends over several days, occupied in the discussion of matters affecting the welfare of the Society at large, and of proposals for the amendment of its general rules. In the interval between the general meetings, the functions of the central body are usually discharged by the President and Committee of Management, under whatever title. Two great Orders distance all the others in importance and number of members—the Independent Order of Oddfellows Manchester Unity, which has 787,962 members, and the Ancient Order of

Foresters, which has 731,542. In stating the method of conducting business, it will be convenient to keep these two Orders in mind, as among Orders generally there is considerable difference in nomenclature and in matters of detail. Some, for example, have no "districts", but only "lodges". We shall use the great Orders as the general model.

Every year a new President is elected, called by the Oddfellows the Grand Master, and by the Foresters the High Court Ranger. The branches, which by the Oddfellows are termed Lodges, by the Foresters are termed Courts. To be the chief of one of these great organizations for a year, freely elected by the votes of all his brethren the delegates, who number several hundreds of individuals, and represent hundreds of thousands of members, is a conspicuous honour.

The President opens the proceedings with an address, in which he recapitulates the matters of importance to the Order which have occurred during his year of office, and refers to such other points of interest to Friendly Societies as he thinks advisable. The Committee of Management, termed by the Oddfellows the Board of Directors, by the Foresters the Executive Council, then present a formal report, which is discussed clause by clause, and its recommendations either adopted, or modified, or rejected.

After all the matters before the meeting have been disposed of, the President and Committee for the next year are elected, and the retiring President inducts his successor into office. During his year of office the new President devotes as much of his time as he can spare to visiting branches in various parts of the country, and encouraging them by his addresses to persevere in sound management, to extend their membership, to carry out any necessary reform, and generally to promote the interests of the Order.

The records published by the two great Orders do not enable us to go back to the commencement of the Victorian Era, when the recent enactment of the Poor-law compelled men to think of self-help; but, so far as they go, they indicate marvellous progress, and it is fair to infer that that progress was in operation in the previous years. Thus, on 1st Jan. 1852, the Manchester Unity had 3219 lodges and 225,194 members. On 1st Jan. 1898 it had 4698 lodges and 787,962 members, being an average increase of 32 lodges and 12,234 members per annum. On 1st Jan. 1865 the amount of funds of the lodges was £1,796,349; on 1st Jan. 1871 it was £2,835,262; on 1st Jan. 1898 it was £8,302,390, an average increase of £173,152 per annum in the first period, and £202,486 in the second. The Foresters' published records go back to 1st Jan. 1845, when they had 1456 courts and 65,909 members; by 1st Jan. 1852 the courts were 1605 and the members 89,875, so that in these respects it had then half the strength of the Manchester Unity; on 1st Jan. 1898 the courts were 4899 and their members 731,442, being an average increase since 1852 of 72 courts and 13,860 members per annum, and raising the Order nearly to a level with the Oddfellows. The amount of the court funds was not ascertained before December, 1870, when it was £1,274,935. In the twenty-seven years since that date, the court funds have increased to £5,119,842, an average of £142,404 per annum. One secret of this remarkable growth is to be found in the fact that in December, 1870, the number of courts having graduated scales of contributions was only 1144 out of 3931, or 29 per cent; now the whole of the courts have adopted the system.

The practical enforcement of this important reform began in 1872, when the number of courts having graduated scales of contribution increased in a single year from 1345 to 2890, or from 34 per cent to 71 per cent of the courts then in existence, a striking instance of the power for good inherent in the annual general meeting of delegates.

A curious point in the history of the Orders previously to the passing of the Act of 1875 is the liability to secession. The hold the central body had on the various branches was so weak that whenever a decision was come to on a matter on which a considerable minority of the branches felt strongly, they would break away and form a new order. This tendency has now been checked by the requirement of the Act, that the conditions of secession shall be expressly provided for in the rules of each branch. The Manchester Unity itself was a secession from a previous order of Oddfellows; other orders of Oddfellows have been derived by secession from the Manchester Unity; the Ancient Foresters originated in a secession from a previous body called the Royal Foresters, and has now practically outlived the body from which it seceded. In some cases secession has taken place in opposition to some wise action of the delegates; in others the better branches have been the seceders.

It is an evidence of the smooth working of the Act of 1875 that, while it has enabled the central bodies of societies to exert their legitimate influence and enforce upon the branches necessary reforms, some of which must have been very unpopular with members of the branches principally affected by them, it has entirely checked the tendency to secession, which now only takes place in isolated cases, either of branches which think themselves strong enough to run alone, or of others which are too far gone to reform.

The requirement that there shall be a fund under the control of the central body to which each branch shall contribute is usually fulfilled by the creation of a fund for the relief of branches in distress. By means of such a fund it has been possible to assist a lodge which had been unfortunate, either as the result of miscalculation or of unfavourable experience of sickness, to right itself, or, if that could not be done, to provide for such of its members as are claimants upon the funds. This arrangement is sometimes spoken of as being so essential a part of the bond of union between the branches as to amount to a federal guarantee of the benefits of each branch, but it is not so. Each branch is financially independent, and must provide for its own liabilities. The relief from the central fund is discretionary, and is, in general, only granted when the lodge has complied with the provisions of the general rules. It does not either in form or effect amount to an assumption by the central body of the whole liabilities of the lodge.

The early village club has developed in another direction into the county society. Many village clubs had obtained the patronage of the gentry and clergy as honorary members. In some cases, these honorary members had taken an active share in the management. Their doing so led to the discovery of weak points in the system, and of the instability arising from the small number of members. The suggestion arose that the county gentry might, by acting together as a central body, and by acting locally as local managers, ensure the establishment of the clubs on sound principles; and by centralizing the risks, might get rid of the liability to fluctuation which necessarily imperils the security of a small local society, however careful its calculation of contributions and benefits may have been. Eminent actuaries were accordingly called in, and elaborate tables of contribution provided to meet the requirements of the members. An honorary fund was raised to meet preliminary expenses and to add to the society's stability, and great care was taken in the investment of the funds. The lines of the institution, combining local management with complete centralization of the funds, were laid down with thoroughness and precision.

Many of the societies so formed have realized the expectations of their founders, and have been successfully and soundly managed; but few of them have become so popular as their carefully-planned system, and the advantages they offer, would have led one to expect. Not one has obtained as members more than a small fraction of the industrial population in its district.

For this several reasons might be assigned. The rates fixed by the actuaries in the interests of soundness have been higher than the villagers could easily afford. The share in the management taken by the honorary members has been more than they care to concede. They have the pardonable weakness of preferring to do things in their own way to having things done for them by other people even in a better way. The element of conviviality and good fellowship is sometimes wanting.

In large towns, the type of village society expanded into a town society, on a large scale, having an office for the transaction of its business, instead of meeting at an inn or school-room. These societies approximated to the county societies in regard to scales of rates and otherwise; but the element of patronage, if present in them at all, was not so to the like extent.

The next step is the formation of a general society in London or some other large city, which practically becomes an insurance office. The element of personal knowledge by the members of each other is almost wholly absent, and hence a great safeguard against fraud is wanting in these societies that the smaller societies possess.

Some of these large general societies have grown out of small beginnings and still retain the peculiar features which led to their gradually becoming attractive to an increasing numbers of members. For example, the largest of the class, the Hearts of Oak Friendly Society, has a system of uniform contributions to cover a great variety of benefits. The contribution is not absolutely fixed, but varies by levy, according to the claims made upon the society during the previous quarter. It averages 10*s*. or 10*s*. 6*d*. per quarter, and covers sick benefits, burial money, allowance on birth of child, assurance of tools against fire, and other allowances, some of them on a liberal scale. It does not provide medical attendance, and hence has arisen a practice of forming subsidiary medical clubs in certain localities. Another outgrowth of the large society has been the formation of clubs for the purpose of organizing the election of delegates, arising from the circumstance that the members, being generally unknown to each other, are unable to judge of the merits of the candidates.

The National Deposit Friendly Society, which grew out of a local society at Albury, under the patronage of the Duke of Northumberland, and was by the energy of the late Canon Portal extended first over a county and then over a considerable part of the country, especially in the southern districts, has become a society of this class, established in London, and the special features of this and other Deposit Friendly Societies may now be mentioned.

They are based on a system which combines the features of a Friendly Society with those of a Savings-bank, and was invented by the late Hon. and Rev. Samuel Best, who established a society in the village of Abbotts' Ann, Hampshire, where he was rector. Their legal constitution was provided for under the Act of 1875 (now s. 42 of the Act of 1896) as societies which provide for accumulating at interest, for the use of any member, any surplus of his contributions to the funds of the society or branch which may remain after providing for any assurance in respect of which they are paid, and which provide for the withdrawal of the accumulations. Before 1875 these societies had been legalized by an authority of the Secretary of State.

Out of each member's payment, which he is encouraged to make as large as he can, a certain sum is taken towards the benefit funds of the society, the remainder being credited to him as his own bank or deposit. When he falls ill, a certain proportion of the sick pay fixed when he became a member, upon a scale varying with his age and other circumstances, is taken out of the benefit fund, the remainder he can draw from his own account. When his own account is exhausted, the allowance from the benefit fund also ceases, subject to a provision for a limited allowance of grace pay out of a special fund. When the member arrives at old age, his bank is converted into a pension, which will of course be the larger the more he has saved and the less he has claimed by sickness. The element of insurance in the contract is so small that there is no fear of insolvency, and no necessity for valuation; on the other hand, a member who suffers from prolonged sickness may find the relief of the society fail him through the exhaustion of his own bank at a time when he most wants it.

Akin to these societies in some respects, though widely different in others, are the Dividing Societies, which exist in great numbers, under a variety of names, as Slate Clubs, Tontines, Birmingham Benefit Societies, &c. These also were legalized in 1875 by a provision that no society should be disentitled to registry by reason of a rule for or practice of dividing any part of its funds, if the rules of the society contain distinct provision for meeting all claims upon the society existing at the time of division before any such division takes place.

Previously to 1875 such societies existed in great numbers, as they do now, but they either remained unregistered, or omitted all mention of the practice of dividing from their rules, or steered a middle course by stating that the division should be subject to the provisions of the Friendly Societies Acts.

When societies of a particular form are established in great number in many parts of the country, without regarding whether the form is the one prescribed or encouraged by law, it is to be inferred that there is something in that form of society which especially meets the wishes and conduces to the interests of its members, and the wise legislator will inquire whether his own views are not too narrow, and whether there may not be something in the form of society which deserves the encouragement of the law.

It seems a common mistake on the part of legislators that it is within their province to find out for the people that which is for their good and that which is not, to encourage them to follow the former, and to devise brave punishments for those who will persist in following the latter. This is an absolute error: the province of the legislature is to find out what contracts people desire to enter into, and, when they have entered into them, to see that they fulfil them; not to tell them what contracts they ought to enter into, and what contracts they ought not to enter into. The administrators of the law may not be going beyond their province in offering such advice and guidance as experience may have shown to be useful; but, in general, people are the best judges of their own affairs, and know their own interests better than the wisest statesman who ever made a blunder—and no statesman ever did anything who did not do that. Hence the circumstance that Dividing Societies are popular leads to the conclusion that it is not without reason that they are so. They possess the advantage, that, as a member gets back his surplus payments at the end of the year, he is willing to pay more than the member of a society which looks forward only to the dim and distant future. They have also the advantage, that they frankly provide only for such sickness and death as may occur in the course of the current year. There is no affectation of providing for old age, either directly or indirectly. If the members feel it their duty to provide for old age, they know they must go elsewhere to do so. There is no pretence that they thought their Slate Club would do it for them. Statesmen have moved on several occasions for returns of the number of paupers in workhouses who have been members of Friendly Societies. Such returns have always been misleading, because they have included those who have been members of Dividing Friendly Societies. On the other hand, these societies have obvious disadvantages. So long as it continues a law of nature that the liability to sickness and death increases with age, so long a club that wipes off the slate each year the transactions of the year will find the increase of age of its members a disadvantage. The younger men will refuse to join when they find that the club contains an undue proportion of older men. The older men will find the burden too heavy if there are no younger ones to share it with them. Pleasant, therefore, as the annual dividend may be, and attractive as the working of a "Tontine" may be during its earlier years, it is not to be looked upon as a permanent provision, and the wise workman will not waste his dividend, but will so apply it as to form a provision for the time when the Slate Club ceases to be available.

Another class of Friendly Society has grown up in an interesting manner. For many years village clubs and lodges have had excellent relations with the local doctor. For a small payment by each man, whether well or ill, the doctor has undertaken to attend the members when they are ill, to watch over the interests of the society, and to examine candidates for membership on admission. In the larger towns a modification of this arrangement became possible. By all the clubs combining their medical funds together, a considerable staff of medical men could be retained, and the members of each club could be allowed their choice among them. Everyone knows how largely the personality of the doctor affects his patients, to whom he seeks to be a friend as well as a medical adviser, and accordingly how everything that tends to give freedom of choice between doctor and patient is an advantage. A third development has taken place. The combination of the medical funds of the various clubs into one has in many places raised a fund sufficient to retain the whole services of one or more qualified medical men, and to establish a dispensary house, where the medical officers reside. The relation of the medical men so appointed to the societies which employ them becomes entirely different from that of the old-fashioned club doctor, and hence some friction has arisen between friendly societies and the medical profession. It is alleged that persons make use of these medical aid associations who are in receipt of an income which ought to enable them to consult their own doctor and pay him his proper fees, and that thus the desire of the medical profession to co-operate with Friendly Societies and accept low fees has been abused. It is also alleged that some of the medical aid associations canvass for members, and thus involve their medical officers in unprofessional practices. It is moreover alleged that the salaries paid to the medical officers are so low as to amount to "sweating".

Where the medical associations are merely a combination of existing Friendly Societies and branches for the purpose of obtaining medical aid, we think they are but little open to these complaints. It is true that members of such societies, being thrifty, careful men, often get on in life, and yet desire to retain their membership and their interest in the societies, but such men are not likely to take advantage of the benefits of the medical association, though they have to contribute to its funds; and the circumstance that to qualify for membership of the medical association, a man must be already a member of a friendly society, in which his interest is much greater, disposes of the risk of canvassing; while in regard to mere underpayment, the societies are generally willing to meet their medical officers fairly. The associations which are most open to these complaints are those which admit the public generally to their benefits, and thus become essentially trading concerns. These are in general established under other acts than the

Friendly Societies Act, to the benefits of which they can hardly be said to be entitled. As this distinction becomes more clear, it is to be hoped that the excellent relations between Friendly Societies and the medical profession will be re-established. The prosperity of a Friendly Society so largely depends upon having as its medical adviser one who will safeguard its funds by his vigilance over claims for sick pay, and will use his professional skill to restore the health of the members as quickly as may be, that anything which raises a cloud between the societies and the medical men is greatly to be regretted.

The Act of 1875 provided that no person should be a member of a society under the age of 16 years, except in a society consisting wholly of persons above the age of 3 years and under the age of 16. The Act of 1887 allowed the societies so constituted to extend the maximum age to 21. As, however, no person can be a trustee, treasurer, or member of the committee of management of any society who is under the age of 21 years, the juvenile societies created under these enactments present the anomaly of being societies which are incapable of being self-managed, and are thus a wholly exceptional class, as the guiding principle of the act is the self-management of societies. This has had one curious consequence—that as sickness and death are relatively infrequent between the ages of 3 and 21, these separate juvenile societies have sometimes accumulated considerable funds, which, as the members cease to belong to them at a given age, remain unclaimed. It would appear from legal decisions, that such unclaimed funds are *bona vacantia* and belong to the Crown. The Act of 1895 put an end to all the anomalies incident to juvenile societies by enacting that every society may have members at any age exceeding one year. In order to facilitate the termination of the separate existence of juvenile societies, and to ensure the just application of their funds, the same act provided a simple machinery for the amalgamation of a juvenile society with an ordinary society or branch, or for the distribution of the members among several branches. It is to be hoped that by this means an end may speedily be put to these utterly anomalous bodies: but the conservatism of the working-man is so great that as yet there is a strong disinclination to adopt the simple method of the act for doing so.

Chapter V.

Burial Societies.

The groups of societies which have been discussed in the last chapter have been those which have for their principal object the assurance of sick pay, to which funeral allowance, relief in distress, and other benefits are secondary. There is a large class of societies which assure no sick pay but only burial money, and as the more important of these are regulated by a special statute, it will be convenient to consider them in a separate chapter. We have already referred in Chapter III. to the origin of this form of society.

The Burial Societies of all classes are to be distinguished from other societies by the smallness of the interest of each member, by the circumstance that a large proportion of the members are young children, and that, in comparison with the members of other societies, the members are not so well off in a financial point of view, nor so well educated. For all these reasons, the member of a burial society does not count for so much as the member of an ordinary friendly society.

A number of the Burial Societies are local. The towns of Preston, Macclesfield, Blackburn, and Chorley have many societies of this class, and in Manchester, Salford, and other large places in Lancashire and the north they are also frequent. They usually employ collectors, but the collectors only work within the limits of the town, and in some cases the collectors are themselves members. The expenses of management are not unduly heavy, and the societies fulfil a requirement that is felt very strongly by those who join them. It is not to be doubted that the provision of burial money is an object that is very important to those whose income is too small to meet the expenses caused by death in a family, and that their sentiments are greatly concerned in being able to render the last offices of respect to the dead, and being saved the humiliation and indignity of having to leave to the parish the duty of burying the remains of those to whom they were attached in life.

The existence of this sentiment has resulted also in the formation of societies, counting their "members" by the million, extending their operations over the whole of the United Kingdom, and employing an army of collectors, under the command of well-paid officers. These societies are known as "collecting societies", and all such as have been registered since 1st Jan. 1896 are required to adopt "Collecting Society" as the last words of the registered name. The provisions of the Friendly Societies Act apply to such of the societies as are registered under it; and those of the "Collecting Societies and Industrial Insurance Companies Act 1896" apply to all collecting societies, whether registered or unregistered, and to all industrial insurance companies which receive contributions by means of collectors on a similar system. The requirements of this act are that every member or person insured is to have a copy of the rules and a printed and signed policy, at a cost not exceeding one penny for each; that before the society can take advantage of any forfeiture for non-payment of contributions, it must give fourteen days' notice to the member and allow him the opportunity of paying the amount; that a member is not to be handed over from one society to another without his written consent; that notice is to be given to the members of general meetings and of any proposed amendment of rules; that the balance-sheets are to be open for inspection during seven days before the annual meeting is held, and are to be certified by a professional accountant, as well as by the auditors; that disputes may be settled by the County Court or the magistrate for the place where the member or claimant lives; that collectors are not to hold office on the committee of management, or vote, or take part in the proceedings of meetings; and that all these provisions of the Act are to be set forth in the rules of the Societies. The members are thus in possession of information as to their rights in respect of management, and are protected, if they choose to avail themselves of the protection, against some of the practices which were alleged to have been carried on by these societies before the Act of 1875 was passed.

It will be seen that in the nature of things the individual member must be of small account in the management of such a society. It becomes in fact an insurance company, without any capital or body of shareholders. In two of the largest of these societies a remedy for this has been sought to be provided by the establishment of a system of delegates, elected at local meetings held in every place where there are a sufficient number of members to claim representation. So far this system appears to have worked fairly well. One main objection to this class of society lies in the expense incurred. Out of the small contributions paid by members, nearly half is absorbed in expenses of management. The labour of collecting small contributions from house to house is no doubt very great, and the collectors have to get through a large amount of work in order to earn a living wage: at the same time, the circumstance that a collector's "book" is a saleable commodity, for which a considerable sum can be obtained, seems to indicate that the collectors are not underpaid. It is a rather curious incident of this class of business that the "good-will" of it, as represented by the "book", is treated as the property of the collector, and not of the society. In the rules of some societies, an attempt is made to control these transactions of sale and purchase, but it is generally recognized that the sale is for the benefit of the collector. Hence arises that paramount influence of the collector in the affairs of the society which the legislature has endeavoured to check. In a large society, the management fund leaves a margin also for liberal remuneration to the chief officers. A society into which the Hon. E. Lyulph Stanley held an inspection some years ago, had two general secretaries, who each received between £5000 and £6000 a-year salary. The existence of rich prizes like this led to continual conflicts in the meetings between the body in possession, who naturally desired to retain their emoluments, and expectant bodies outside, who equally naturally wished to enjoy a share in them. This, and the circumstance that the emoluments increased with the business done, led to grave mischiefs in the management, of which Mr. Stanley records some remarkable instances. The meetings were often scenes of disturbance, and many illegalities and irregularities took place.

The result of Mr. Stanley's investigation was that the two managing secretaries resigned their position, which may be taken as an indication that there was good ground for setting the investigation on foot. Various reforms were made in the procedure of the society, and Mr. Stanley himself consented to become a trustee of it, and has thus been able to watch over the manner in which these reforms have been carried into effect.

These reforms, however, only to a moderate degree affect the great difficulty of dealing with societies of this class, arising from the unavoidably high expense of management. The question has often been asked—Can no other machinery be devised by which the benefits of burial assurance can be obtained for the great body of the industrial population at a less expense? Cannot the Post-office, or some other Government department, undertake to do the work at a less cost? We think that the answer must necessarily be in the negative, so long as the insurers insist upon their contributions being collected from them at their own homes. In the majority of cases it is the mother who transacts the business with the collector, and saves up and pays to him the few pence which insure her own and her husband and children's funeral money. She will not go to the Post-office to pay it, and the Post-office, if it is to do the same business which is now done by the collecting society, must go to her. That possibly might be done without great additional cost if she were a person having a large correspondence, but she is of a class the postman rarely visits, and a special collecting postman would have to be put on for her. More than this—the collector who receives the money, and thus makes a saleable "book", earns the value of his book by the arts of persuasion which he uses upon these poor mothers to induce them to effect the insurances; and the special postman, if he is to be a success, would have to learn to use the same arts of persuasion, and would thus become as much unlike the ordinary government officer as could be.

The Collecting Societies Act extends also to Industrial Assurance Companies. These differ from the Collecting Societies in having a more or less numerous body of shareholders among whom the profits of the business are divided. The largest of them is the Prudential Assurance Company, which can boast of having upon its books about one-third of the whole population of the country. It has in existence 13 million policies, and its accumulated funds amount to £30,438,000. It need hardly be said that its shareholders are very fortunate persons.

There are two points in respect of this group of societies and companies which are worthy of consideration: the first is, that there seems reason to believe that many persons are insured repeatedly in one and another office, and frequently the persons effecting, or hoping to profit by the insurance are persons who have no real insurable interest in the life. The legal consequence of this is that such policies are void; but as the forfeiture would be in favour of the society or company, this does not operate to prevent the contract being entered upon, and the society or company rarely avails itself of the defence, on account of the unpopularity and loss of business that would follow. It is greatly to be feared, therefore, that illegal insurances are frequently effected.

The second is, that a considerable portion of the profit

made by these societies and companies arises from the lapsing of policies. That was the case in earlier times with all assurance companies; but the ordinary policy-holder now knows his rights, and rarely suffers a valuable policy to lapse. In industrial assurance companies the policy-holders are still in the early stage, and policies are frequently allowed to lapse after they ought to have acquired a surrender value.

In the Collecting Society, father, mother, and all children above one year of age count as separate members. The great extension of this practice of the insurance of children has led to grave apprehensions as to its effect on infant mortality. In a few cases, convictions for child-murder have been obtained, and it has been shown that the burial money has been an inducement to the crime. The same thing might be said of ordinary insurance. We think it would be a libel on the great body of the population who are members of burial societies to say that they are so sordid and so false to parental instinct as to wilfully kill their children for the purpose of enjoying the small sum of burial money for which they have been insured. If such a horrid practice prevailed, it would be in the interests of the societies themselves to stop it. There is no evidence that it does prevail. The members of burial societies are so poor that a small sum appears large to them, and the burial money comes as a consolation when a child is lost. The lines of Clough have been quoted in this connection:

> "Thou shalt not kill, but needst not strive
> Officiously to keep alive".

Whether a tendency to neglect may not be sometimes unconsciously fostered by the existence of the burial money contract may be questioned.

The legislature has endeavoured to meet this by some stringent provisions as to payments on the death of children under ten:—

1. The money is not to be paid to anybody but the parent, or the personal representative of the parent who survived. It is to be feared that some societies interpret the term "personal representative" with laxity, and it is certain that insurances are sometimes effected by persons other than the parent.
2. The sum to be assured or paid on the death of a child under five years of age is not to exceed £6. This seems a larger sum than necessary, and the House of Lords in 1875 amended it to £3; but this amendment was disagreed with by the House of Commons when the bill returned to that house.
3. On the death of a child between five and ten, £10 may be insured.
4. Where the child is insured in more than one office, the total insurances must not exceed these limits.
5. No payment is to be made except upon production of a special certificate from the registrar of deaths.
6. The registrar is to state in the certificate the name of the society to which it is to be produced, and the amount of the claim said to be due from it.
7. Where he grants more than one certificate, he shall number them consecutively, and the total amount of claim for which he issues them is not to exceed the limits.
8. He is not to issue a certificate unless the cause of death is medically certified, or other satisfactory evidence of the cause is furnished.
9. The society is to inquire what sums have been paid

by other societies when the certificate does not purport to be the first.

Cases have arisen which show that these provisions require strengthening. It should be observed that they apply to all Friendly Societies, whether registered or unregistered, and to Industrial Assurance Companies and Trade-unions. Industrial Assurance Companies and registered Friendly Societies are exempted from the provisions of the Life Assurance Act 1774, which render void all insurances where the person insuring has no interest in the life insured.

Deplorable instances of fraud have occurred in Collecting Societies, in some of which the perpetrators have been prosecuted to conviction. In the absence of fraud, there ought not to be much risk of these societies becoming insolvent, inasmuch as their premiums are ample to cover the benefits insured. If the rates charged are compared with those of an ordinary insurance company, it will be seen that, even after allowance is made for the heavy expenditure of the Collecting Society, there is a considerable margin left in the premium for profit.

It has accordingly been suggested that where a society of this class shows a balance deficient, there should be vested in some authority the power compulsorily to wind it up, inasmuch as the existence of the deficiency is in itself proof of mismanagement, and affords strong presumption of fraud. Nothing in the statutes, however, deals with these societies on any footing other than that of voluntary action, and the registrar has no more authority to institute proceedings of a compulsory character against societies of this class than against societies of any other class. In each case, he must be moved to action by the members themselves. It is true that while in a society of less than a thousand members, it requires one-fifth of the whole number to set him in motion, in a society of 1000 or more, 100; and in a society of more than 10,000 members, 500 can do so. Except through the medium of the collectors, 500 signatures cannot easily be obtained, and therefore such applications are frequently set on foot by dissatisfied collectors, and become only incidents in the chronic struggle between those who are in the management to keep there, and those who are out of it to get in. It is rarely that the registrar is called upon to act by the spontaneous impulse of the members themselves. For the reasons that have been already given, they have not sufficient interest in the society to be moved to such action, and they have not the means of combination. Yet, in many cases, these powers of the registrar have been usefully exercised—as in the case of the inspection of the Royal Liver Society, conducted by Mr. Lyulph Stanley; the special meetings of the Royal Liver, the Scottish Legal, and the Liverpool United, or Royal Oak, in each of which a change in the system of management had become necessary, and precautions were taken to ensure order at the meetings, and to secure that the sense of the members was taken. In other cases, as that of the Independent Mutual Brethren, where the insolvency of the concern was evident, an application by members for an award of dissolution enabled a complete investigation to be made into the frauds which had led to the disaster.

Chapter VI.

Financial Position of Friendly Societies.

For the person who desires to join a Friendly Society it is not sufficient that he should understand the peculiarities of its constitution. It is much more important that he should know something about its financial condition. The man who joins an insolvent society is aptly described by the sarcastic words of the prophet Haggai, "He that earneth wages, earneth wages to put it into a bag with holes".

The first point to be considered is the nature of the contract of insurance against sickness. Sickness, in the language of Friendly Societies, does not denote merely a pathological condition. It means inability to work, produced by disease or infirmity. In some cases it extends to both bodily and mental disorder, and to infirmity produced by lameness, blindness, insanity, &c. In other cases it is limited to inability to work produced by acute bodily disease.

It follows that sickness which does not cause inability to work does not constitute a claim on a Friendly Society. The occupation of the member thus becomes a material element; inasmuch as men of one occupation may continue able to work at it during an illness that would disable men of another occupation. There is also the moral consideration, that a man of firm mind and industrious temperament will continue at work, when a man of weak, flabby, and lazy disposition would lie up for the same disorder.

It is clear from this that no model tables derived from the experience of other societies will of themselves ensure the solvency of a society; and this is one of the many reasons why the legislature has wisely refrained from prescribing model tables, or from accepting any responsibility for the terms of the contracts that members of Friendly Societies enter into. Any other policy would be a distinct encouragement to the lazy as against the industrious, and to laxity of administration as against care. It could not be carried out with safety unless the State took upon itself the whole management of the societies, and reduced them to a Government department.

It is nevertheless essential that a society should charge sufficient and equitable rates of premium for the benefits that it assures: for though they cannot of themselves secure success, independently of careful administration, good management of itself would be of no avail if the rates of contribution were insufficient or inequitable.

Those who were interested in Friendly Societies saw from a very early stage in their working that the only way to ascertain what were the proper contributions to be charged for sick pay would be to tabulate the experience of the societies themselves, and to do so on a scale so large that the errors of one society in paying too much might be corrected by those of another society in paying too little. The first important attempt of this kind was made by the Highland Society in 1824. By offering prizes for the best returns, it obtained information from seventy societies in Scotland, and its observations included more than 100,000 individuals.

In 1835 Mr. Ansell published the results of a similar collection of information made by the Society for the Diffusion of Useful Knowledge.

Meanwhile the Act of Parliament had been passed which required every Friendly Society once in every five years to make a return, in a prescribed form, of the sickness and mortality it had experienced. The returns thus collected for the five years 1836–40 were intrusted to Mr. F. G. P. Neison the elder, who published the abstracts in a work called *Vital Statistics*. He distinguished them into rural, town, and city districts: the rural districts having greatly the advantage of the others in respect both of sickness and mortality.

In 1850 the Corresponding Secretary of the Manchester Unity of Oddfellows, Mr. Henry Ratcliffe, published a Return of the Sickness and Mortality experienced by the Lodges of that Order. This also was distinguished into rural, town, and city districts. He issued a second series of tables in 1862, and a third series in 1872. This latter included 1,321,000 years of life, and was adopted by the Treasury in the regulations made for the guidance of Public Valuers as the standard table to be used by them pending the preparation of tables from the quinquennial returns from 1856 to 1880.

The quinquennial returns to 1850 were abstracted in 1854 by Mr. A. G. Finlaison, the actuary to the Commissioners for the Reduction of the National Debt, who prepared a series of tables from them, in which he excluded cases of chronic and prolonged sickness, so that the tables were not available for societies which granted allowances during such sickness, and thus Ratcliffe's tables were preferred. The subdivision adopted was into light labour and heavy labour.

In 1896 the largest series of observations yet made was published in a blue book of 1367 folio pages. It is based on the quinquennial returns from 1856 to 1880, and was prepared by Mr. W. Sutton, the Actuary to the Registry of Friendly Societies. The tables are based upon the experience of 4,480,809 years of life.

They are divided into five groups, the result of the returns for males from 1856 to 1860, 1861 to 1870, 1876 to 1880 being given separately, and also those for females, and for males in Wales, representing the mining districts. With regard to the group of males, 1876 to 1880, representing 1,662,562 years of life, a subdivision is effected into five smaller groups, according to the population of the places where the registered offices of the societies are respectively situate, so that those in places having a population under 2000, between 2000 and 7000, between 25,000 and 100,000, and above 100,000 can be distinguished. In order that societies may have the means of ascertaining the value of every variety of liability which they are in the habit of undertaking, separate values are given for every four weeks of sickness during the first year of sickness, for each half of the second year, and for three years and upwards. From these the value of every combination of full pay, half pay, and reduced pay can be ascertained.

It may be stated generally that, as compared with previous observations, these tables give an increased liability to sickness. Whether this arises from the fact that sickness claims are actually increasing in Friendly Societies, or that previous observation consisted mainly of societies which had had a favourable experience, or from some other cause, it is not easy to determine.

The tables indicate, among other things, the extreme importance of the rate of interest. The liabilities for sick pay of a society consisting of members of 30 years of age which could invest its funds at 4 per cent would be, in present money, £43, 14*s.* 10*d.* for every £1 a week sick pay insured: those of a society which could only obtain 2½ per cent on its investments would be, in present money, £65, 11*s.*, or almost half as much again.

The several collections of observations to which we have referred differ in many minor points, but they all agree in one—that the liability to sickness, in the Friendly-Society sense of the word, increases with age, slowly at first, between the ages of 20 and 40, afterwards more rapidly, and that as men reach the more advanced ages the increase becomes so great that it is practically not to be distinguished from a pension. In other words, that an age comes when man is not able to work any longer, and that age is approached by a gradual increase of the length of time during which man, on the average, is unable to work.

Now, if we remember that the primary object of a Friendly Society is to provide for such inability to work through sickness as may occur to any man in the best years of his working life, and that it is only a secondary object to provide for that inability to work which must come to every man sooner or later after those best years are over, we shall see that there is a great practical advantage in keeping those two ideas separate.

There are many ways of providing for old age; but there is no other way of providing for the casual sickness which for the time dries up all the sources of income, and adds its own burdens of expenditure, than that offered by the Friendly Society. If the assurance against sickness is limited to the years of working life, the amount of funds required to be accumulated by the society for future years will not be so large as if the assurance is continued during old age. Some accumulation will be necessary; because the liability to sickness during the years from 40 to 65 is much greater than the liability to sickness during the years from 20 to 40, and the contribution must be so fixed as to be sufficient for both.

The contribution, therefore, which every member pays to the sick fund of his Friendly Society may be divided into two parts—the one, that which corresponds to the actual sickness which he and other members of the same age experience on the average during the current year; the other, that which is to be accumulated so as to provide for the sickness of future years. As time goes on, the first part of the contribution becomes larger and larger, till it leaves nothing for the second part, and then the member has to draw upon his accumulation. Assuming, for the sake of illustration, that a society consisted wholly of persons of the same age, and that sick pay and contributions both ceased at the age of 65, then the amount accumulated at the end of the sixty-fourth year of age of the members, and their contributions during the sixty-fifth year, would (if the society had worked out according to the tables on which its contributions were calculated) exactly equal the sickness experienced during that year, and at the end of the year the last week's sick pay would be paid to the last member sick out of the contributions of the last members not sick, and the sick fund would come to an end. If, however, the sick pay and contributions were not to cease at 65, but to continue throughout the whole of life, then at the end of the members' sixty-fifth year of age it would be necessary for the society to have still in hand a large sum, representing the probable excess of the sick claims over the contributions during the whole remainder of the lives of the members; and thus it is easily to be seen that to insure sick pay during the whole of life would require a much larger contribution and a much longer continuance of accumulation than to assure sick pay for a limited time only.

The supposition that all the members are of the same

age has only been used for simplicity of illustration. It does not occur in practice. Where the members are of different ages the calculation of the amount of accumulation that the society ought to have, becomes a matter of some difficulty, and the method of effecting it is called a valuation. As the law requires such a valuation to be made once at least in every five years, it is called the Quinquennial Valuation. This is a process which can only be performed by a professional actuary, or by someone who has mastered at least enough of the elements of the actuarial profession to know the meaning of the algebraical formulæ involved.

As the returns of sickness and mortality experience contain a number of auxiliary tables by which these calculations may be made, a general comprehension of the principles of valuation is not difficult of attainment; and it would be very desirable that it should form one of the subjects taught at every public elementary school. As the scholars will be the members of Friendly Societies of the future, nothing could be more useful to them than to be well drilled in the mathematical basis upon which the soundness of those societies rests, and nothing would do more to check the spread of societies formed on the unsound methods of equal rates and periodical division than the dissemination among the young of a real knowledge of the true conditions of sickness assurance.

In the absence of this knowledge, the members of a society, when its funds increase from year to year, sometimes look upon the increase as in itself conclusive evidence that the society is prosperous; but that is not so: the society may be increasing its liabilities to a much greater extent than the increase of its funds, and the test of a valuation may show that it is actually going downhill. So rooted is the idea that the increase of funds must mean prosperity that we have known cases where the members of a society have refused to act upon the report of the valuer, believing that the adverse result which it showed must have been due to a mistake on his part. It would be a most effectual cure for delusions of this kind if the young were taught something of the science of Friendly Society calculations.

There is an error on the other hand that should also be guarded against. The aspect of a valuation is towards the future, not the past. When a valuer declares that such a society has a deficiency of so many thousand pounds, that is not the same thing as saying that somebody has embezzled so many thousand pounds of the society's cash, or that its bank has broken, or its investments been depreciated to the same extent. It does not mean more than this: that if the society continues to carry out its existing contracts without modification, and does not take any measures to improve its position, a deficiency will ultimately accrue, of which the present value is so many thousand pounds.

Assuming that the society took the heroic course of raising the money, which is rarely practicable, the result would be, that if the valuer's estimates should turn out to be confirmed by the actual future experience of the society, and if the society admitted no new members, the last member would receive the last pound, and the society would work itself out. The same result would be obtained by diminishing the future benefits to the extent to which the deficiency represents the present value of such benefits—for example, if the valuer found the present value of the future benefits to be £20,000 and the deficiency to be £5000, the reduction of the future benefit by an average of one-fourth would wipe out the deficiency. It could in like manner be obtained by increasing the future contributions, or by a combination of both methods. The practical skill and competence of the valuer are greatly tested by the measures he recommends the society to adopt for effecting the necessary adjustment.

Some interesting examples may be given of how a valuation deficiency may be met. A society in Warwickshire had a deficiency of £4396. In the course of the next five years it increased its funds from £10,880 to £13,361, and so reduced its benefits that their present value was diminished from £26,024 to £20,922, or nearly 20 per cent (4*s*. in the pound). The result was that the next valuation showed a surplus of £2045. A society in Middlesex was in the apparently hopeless condition that its funds were £3720 only, and its valuation deficiency was £5023. This society took such vigorous steps for increasing its funds and extending its business, upon properly calculated rates of premium, that in five years it had raised its capital to £10,297, and though it had increased the value of its estimated future liabilities from £40,282 to £77,333, the valuation brought out a surplus of £413. A third society, in Surrey, was in a position which even the most heroic measures would hardly have seemed sufficient to retrieve. Its funds were only £3471, yet its estimated valuation deficiency was £18,131. There could be nothing in such a case short of a drastic dealing with the promised benefits, the value of which was reduced in the next valuation from £22,770 to £9874, or more than 56 per cent (11*s*. in the £). The funds were also increased to £4912, and the valuation showed a surplus of £378.

These examples may serve to show that the condition

of valuation "deficiency" is rarely a hopeless condition. We wrote the following words in 1881, and nothing that has since occurred has shown them to be incorrect:— "A word of caution may be added against forming too hasty conclusions adverse to Friendly Societies if it should turn out that the valuations in many cases show an estimated deficiency in the funds to meet the liabilities. It would be strange if it were otherwise when for the first time scientific tests are applied to contracts that have been in operation without a scientific basis for a long series of years. It must be borne in mind, however, that nothing is more elastic than the contract made by a Friendly Society with its members; no error more easy of remedy, if found out in time, than one existing in the original terms of such a contract. Hence the words 'insolvency', 'rottenness', and the like, which we sometimes hear freely used as describing the general condition of Friendly Societies are utterly out of place. Of Friendly Societies in general it may be said that as there are no associations the benefits of which are more important to their members, so there are none that are managed with greater rectitude, and few with equal success."

The recent experience of one of the smaller Orders, but yet an important one, having as many as 1000 branches, is another case in point. Its valuation to 31st December, 1891, showed that on the aggregate of all the branches their assets were only 15*s.* 1*d.* in the £ of their estimated liabilities.

A valuation to 31st December, 1896, showed that in the aggregate of all the branches their assets were 16*s.* 1*d.* in the £ of their estimated liabilities. If it is remembered that a deficiency must increase from year to year unless steps are taken to diminish it, it will be seen that most resolute efforts must have been made during the five years to secure this result, which is the more remarkable that the Order has undergone during that time a very unfavourable experience of sickness. The valuers calculate that, taking all things into consideration, the measures adopted were equivalent to an addition of a quarter of a million to the resources of the Order. It has still much to do to attain complete actuarial solvency, for a deficiency of 3*s.* 11*d.* in the £ is a serious one, but the results here mentioned should encourage the Order to pursue the course of reform it has so successfully commenced.

The elasticity and recuperative power which we have referred to as characteristic of Friendly Societies applies mainly to that branch of their business which deals with assurance against sickness. The assurance of burial money in a Friendly Society differs in no way from life assurance as practised by a company, and the principles of valuation of life policies have been so fully investigated by professional actuaries, and are so familiar to all who take a practical interest in the subject, that it is not necessary to discuss them here. Those who desire to study the question will find all they require in the second volume of the *Institute of Actuaries Text Book.* The assurance of old-age pensions, however, stands on a different footing from that of sick pay, and this lends great force to the argument that a society insuring old-age pensions should place all its contributions for that purpose in a separate fund, and jealously guard every penny of them from even a temporary use for any of the other purposes of the society.

The assurance of sick pay involves the system of brotherly visitation by the members—valuable, on the one hand, as establishing kindly relations between them, and on the other, as a powerful check upon malingering—and develops the element of good-fellowship, which is one of the best features of Friendly Societies. The assurance of a deferred pension involves merely the receipt of the contribution, and the careful accumulation of it at compound interest until the time arrives when the pension begins to be payable.

The assurance of sick pay allows of considerable fluctuations—a year or a few years of heavy experience of sickness will naturally be followed by a similar number of years of light experience of sickness, and the one will counteract the other. The assurance of a pension requires the steady accumulation of the money at compound interest, and offers no means of recovering an amount once lost by bad investment or otherwise. Every pound lost when a man is 20 results in a loss of four pounds when he is 65.

While the assurance of sick pay is best done by the small lodge, where all the members know each other, the assurance of pension would be most safely and conveniently effected through the central body of the whole Order, who would have a large average of lives over which to spread the risk and large funds to invest, so as to prevent the loss that arises from money lying idle. In every respect, therefore, the two kinds of assurance are in strong contrast with each other.

A similar observation applies to assurance of endowments at a fixed age. These depend wholly on the accumulation of the contributions, and therefore should not in any way be mixed up with funds of a more fluctuating character, such as sick pay. There does not seem much necessity for the transaction of endowment business by Friendly Societies, now that the Post Office has made the accumulation of savings so easy:

but every society which grants endowment policies should keep a separate fund for the purpose.

It has been observed as a curious fact that when a society or branch has large funds, there is a tendency to an increase in claims for sick pay, the members perhaps fancying that the society is well able to meet those claims, and having generally large and liberal views; while a society that is poor, is often spared by its members, who also keep a sharper look-out on claims. Thus what Mr. Sutton has called the "personal equation"—in allusion to a well-known problem in mathematics, where the effect of the difference of quickness of observation in different people on the result of the observations is sought to be ascertained—has a great deal to do with the assurance of sick pay. In respect of the assurance of fixed annuities and of endowments, it is almost entirely absent. For this reason, also, it becomes essential that these assurances should be kept apart.

It follows from what has been said, that without a periodical valuation a society has no means whatever of knowing whether it is solvent or insolvent; whether, as years go on, its members will find themselves deprived of its benefits when those benefits are most needed; or whether it is now giving to its members an unfair share of its funds. The mere continuous increase of funds affords no guide whatever to the society's real financial condition. More than fifty years ago the legislature was sufficiently well informed to see that this must be so; and the Act of 1846 required every society to make a return of its assets and liabilities once in every five years. Strangely enough, in 1850 that provision was repealed, before a single term of five years had been completed, so that in this respect the

Act of 1846 was entirely a dead letter. Even in 1855, when the Act was passed which worked so well for twenty years, the lesson which the legislature had learned in 1846 was wholly forgotten; and no provision for periodical valuation was made until 1875. It is clear from the experience that has been gained under the Act of 1875, that if the requirement of a quinquennial valuation contained in the Act of 1846 had not been repealed, but had been enforced during the thirty years' interval, the financial condition of Friendly Societies would at this day have been very different from that revealed by the recent valuations.

Chapter VII.

Other Societies under the Friendly Societies Act.

Several classes of societies, which are not Friendly Societies proper, are admitted to the benefit of the Friendly Societies Act. It will be convenient to consider them here, although they do not follow in the order of succession which has been indicated in the commencement of previous chapters.

Cattle Insurance Societies provide for insurance to any amount against the loss of neat cattle, sheep, lambs, swine, horses, and other animals by death from disease or otherwise. Shortly after the passing of the Act of 1855, the Secretary of State had given authority for the extension of its provisions to societies for assuring the members against loss by disease or death of cattle employed in trade or agriculture, but that was subject to the limitation that no member should contract for a sum payable on any contingency exceeding £200. By an Act passed in 1866, at a time when the rinderpest had been making great ravages, this limitation was repealed so far as relates to such societies; and it was provided that contributions to these societies should be recoverable as a debt. These two distinctions are maintained in the existing law. In other respects, the same provisions relate to Cattle Insurance Societies as to friendly societies, except that no quinquennial valuation is required from them. The extension to "other animals" is due to the Act of 1896. Few of these societies avail themselves of the permission to insure more than £200. The majority of them are small pig clubs and cow clubs, mainly established in and about the county of Lincoln, and doubtless very valuable to their members.

Benevolent Societies are societies for any benevolent or charitable purpose. All the charitable societies of the United Kingdom are capable of being registered under the Friendly Societies Act, and it would be well for many of them if they were so registered. The great abuses that arise in charities for want of a proper audit of accounts might then be remedied. The subscribers would have access to the accounts, and would be able to see to the honest application of their benefactions in a much more thorough way than they can do in the absence of such registry. The simple definition of a Benevolent Society is a society to which the members subscribe not for their own benefit but for the benefit of others. A society from which the members themselves or their families are to derive benefit cannot be registered as a Benevolent Society. Like other registered societies, a Benevolent Society may hold land, but not more than an acre in extent. The privilege of nomination for sums payable at death does not apply to the society, nor can it have a rule for dividing its funds.

Working-men's Clubs. These are societies for purposes of social intercourse, mutual helpfulness, mental and moral improvement, and rational recreation. 452 such clubs, registered in England and Wales, made returns—many of them very imperfect ones—for the year ending 31st December, 1895. The number of members was 116,370, an average of 257 to each. The revenue of the clubs for the year was £325,821, an average of £721, or about £3 per member. 120 of them owed upon mortgage £90,230, or an average of £700 each. 371 of them had accumulated profits amounting to £107,938, or £290 each; 50 had made losses amounting to £3886, or £78 each. The largest club appears to be one at Huddersfield, with 7140 members. The largest revenue returned is that of the Borough of Leicester Club, £5051. This Club has 1631 members, and its accumulated profits are £3170. The largest mortgage indebtedness is that borne by the Bryanston Club, London, £6061. This club has 390 members, £2150 revenue, and £118 profit. The largest profit appears to have been accumulated by a club at Wisbech, with 1136 members and £1818 revenue, which returns its profits at £5901. The losses are small in comparison, the largest being £448, which is returned by the Walworth Radical Club, having 310 members and £1581 revenue. Of the 452 clubs, 74 are in Yorkshire and 68 in Middlesex, these two counties between them having about one-third of the whole number. If Lancashire is thrown in with Yorkshire these two great northern counties have 132; and if Surrey be added to Middlesex, the two metropolitan counties have 110; or, together, considerably more than half the whole number of registered clubs. An interesting group of 7 clubs exists at Swindon, in Wiltshire, mainly among the persons employed by the Great Western Railway. These clubs have together 4882 members and a revenue of £16,808. Four of them have mortgages on their club premises amounting to £4435. About one-fifth of the clubs indicate by their name that they are in connection with a political party, usually the Liberal or Radical, but the promotion of political objects is not a purpose for which a working-man's club is allowed to be established under the Friendly Societies Act. Eleven of the clubs are brass and other bands, the practice of such bands being undoubtedly a form of rational recreation. Their registry enables them to protect their property in the instruments and music, some of which are costly, acquired by them for the use of their members. Several clubs represent combinations of the members of the various Friendly Societies in a district, and afford, beside the other advantages of a club, a convenient place of meeting for such societies and their branches.

The Working-man's Club, at any rate as it was originally devised, and is now in the majority of cases actually carried on, deserves all the protection and encouragement that the Friendly Societies Act can give it, though it differs from the ordinary Friendly Society in not insuring any actual money benefits. The powers and facilities of the Act were first extended to clubs on the 27th January, 1864, by authority of the Secretary of State, and among the purposes stated in that authority was that of affording facilities for the meetings of Friendly Societies legally established. It was thus one of the original ideas of their promoters that there should be a link between them and Friendly Societies. The principal originator of these clubs, and founder of the

Working-men's Club and Institute Union, a body which promotes their establishment and assists them with advice and model rules, and also by the settlement of disputes, and makes provision for intercommunication between them, was the late Rev. Henry Solly, and to him and Mr. Hodgson Pratt, a gentleman of well-known benevolence, the clubs are much indebted. In their primitive form, they no doubt had more of the institute than the club element, but their founders very soon learned that a Working-man's Club, to be successful, must give its members relatively to their means the same comforts and amenities that form the attraction of a West End Club to its members. It was seen that the providing of games and even of alcoholic refreshments would not necessarily encourage gambling or drunkenness. In this matter, however, precautions had to be taken. The Inland Revenue authorities had to be satisfied as to the genuineness of the club, and as to its advantages being limited to those who were actual members. This was done by the adoption of a rule, stringently prohibiting any payment for an excisable commodity being made by any visitor to the club, a rule which many clubs enforce by fine and expulsion against a member who introduces a visitor and allows him to pay for anything. Upon an undertaking being given that this rule shall be adopted and rigorously enforced, the Working-men's Club is put in the same position as any other club, its members providing themselves as a body with the supplies that they dispense at a price to themselves as individuals.

Thus understood, as a means of providing for working-men the pleasures of social intercourse and some of the comforts of life by means of combination, Working-men's Clubs may fairly be included among Provident

Societies; but it will be easily seen that the absolute freedom from restraint enjoyed by a club member, his right when once within the walls of his club to treat it as a home and to be supplied with what he wants from its stores at any hour or on any day, may lead to abuse. When clubs are found to be crowded at the hours when public-houses are shut, and comparatively empty at other times, they certainly have a mischievous tendency. It has been observed, moreover, that when the hours of opening of public-houses have been restricted in a locality, as at the time of the passing of the Welsh Sunday-closing Act, a crop of clubs has sprung up. In cases like these, a so-called Working-men's Club becomes a mere expedient for evading the licensing acts. It has been so regarded by the magistrates in many places, and convictions have been obtained against the managers. Where that occurs in a club which has been registered, it involves the cancelling of the registry, upon the ground that the club exists for an unlawful purpose; but in general it occurs in clubs that have not been registered. The registrar is called upon to exercise some vigilance in registering clubs, to see that the conditions of membership are genuine, and that its management is confided to a responsible committee, as otherwise he would be registering to-day a body the registry of which he would have to cancel to-morrow; but in the absence of local knowledge he cannot decline to register a club which adopts rules that on the face of them are satisfactory, though they may conceal an intention of illegality, and will be actually disregarded in practice. Upon this ground, that it is impossible for a registrar in London to obtain the knowledge of what goes on in the country that would be requisite to enable him to exercise any effectual control over clubs, we have recommended to the Royal Commission on the Liquor Laws that some other measures of obtaining that control should be devised. The matter is now under the consideration of that body, and their report will no doubt throw much light on a difficult question. It ought to be added, that whenever the registry office has felt called upon to make local inquiries, it has received the readiest assistance from the authorities connected with local government and from the police. Upon the whole, the returns show that so far as regards registered Working-men's Clubs, the probabilities are in favour of good management and against abuse.

A variety of miscellaneous societies have been authorized by the Lords of the Treasury to be registered as for purposes to which, in their lordships' opinion, the provisions of the Friendly Societies Act, or some of them, ought to be extended, and these are called Specially Authorized Societies. The first and most popular specially authorized purpose is 'to create funds by monthly or other subscriptions to be lent out or invested for the members of the society or for their benefit, pursuant to the Friendly Societies Act'. Under this authority a large number of Loan Societies or Money Clubs have been registered. An act is still in force, dating as far back as 1840 (which repealed one passed in 1835), for the establishment of Loan Societies in England and Wales, as to which we shall have something to say in a later chapter; but this act is limited to loans under £15, and does not extend to Scotland or Ireland. In Ireland a number of Loan Societies had been registered under the Friendly Societies Act, and in England Money Clubs had been formed in many places under various titles, but not registered under any act. Without interfering, therefore, with the operation of the act of 1840, this special authority has given a legal constitution to societies which would otherwise have had none. The limitations which affect these societies are those specified in section 46 of the Act of 1896: that a member shall not be capable of holding any interest in the funds exceeding £200, that no loan is to be made to a member exceeding £50, and that the society shall not hold on deposit from members more than two-thirds of the total sums owing by members who have borrowed. The society may in each case fix a lower limit by its rules. The membership of persons under twenty-one years of age is not allowed in these societies, and they are not entitled to exemption from stamp duty and some other privileges. On the other hand, their contributions are made recoverable as a debt, and the right of nomination for payment of sums at death is extended to the members. The Loan Societies Act strictly limits the rate of interest that may be charged to a member, and forbids the imposition of fines or forfeitures upon him; but a specially authorized Loan Society is not under any restriction in either respect, except the general restriction that all fines must be reasonable. In some of these societies the advances are sold to the members for the highest price that any member will offer, by a kind of auction; in others, the repayments are of fixed amount. In some, a yearly division of the whole fund takes place; in others, a yearly division of profit only.

Some societies of this class have branches. An interesting group of these societies is denominated "Self-help Societies", and combines with the loan-society purpose that of relieving members in distressed circumstances. Another group is that of Agricultural Credit Societies, established with a view of introducing into this country a modification of the Raiffeisen system of credit banks, which has been very successful in Italy and other parts of the continent of Europe. In regard to these, it has been found that the provision of the Friendly Societies Act, by which deposits can be received only from members, has hampered their operations, and the Rt. Hon. Mr. Plunkett, who has rendered great service to Ireland by the establishment of Co-operative Dairies, as well as of Agricultural Credit Societies, has obtained in 1898 an Act to confer upon these latter the power of borrowing and receiving deposits from any person, whether members or not, including corporate and other public bodies. The Congested Districts Board is willing to assist such societies in the parts of Ireland over which its operations extend. In order that the bill may not alter the constitution of other societies registered under the same special authority, it is expressly limited to such societies as prohibit their members from making any profit or receiving any dividend, and reserve to the managing body of the society the right of seeing that every loan to a member is applied by the member to a purpose of which the society approves. These are the particular features of the Agricultural Credit Bank, by which all the members undertake to be jointly responsible for any advance made, in the event of the borrower failing to repay it, and in return enforce on the borrower the application of the advance to some agricultural improvement by which it will repay itself. In both these respects it is clearly to be distinguished from the ordinary Money Club.

Societies for assisting members out of employment are also specially authorized. They differ from Trade-unions in not desiring to impose any restrictive conditions on the conduct of any trade or business, but merely to relieve their members while unable to obtain employment. Several such societies have been established in large towns for the benefit of clerks and warehousemen. They usually combine with the specially authorized purpose the objects of an ordinary Friendly Society, but they do not even in that case obtain the special privileges of Friendly Societies.

The protecting and defending members of any trade or calling against frivolous, vexatious, or malicious prosecutions, and in cases of robbery or other crimes affording them legal or other assistance for the detection and prosecution of the offenders, is another object for which a specially authorized society may be registered. Such societies have been established in connection with the occupation of driver of a public conveyance, and other like callings.

Promoting agriculture and horticulture, by obtaining small estates and distributing them in allotments among the members, and by offering prizes and otherwise, is also a purpose to which the Treasury has extended the powers and facilities of the Act. The simplification of title to land resulting from the provisions vesting it in the trustees of the society for the time being without conveyance renders the Act especially favourable to small provident ventures of this kind.

Promoting thrift among the labouring classes by affording them the opportunity of depositing their savings and receiving interest on the same is another specially authorized object. Under this authority penny banks may obtain a legal constitution. The Yorkshire Penny Bank is registered as a company limited by guarantee; but many smaller penny banks in various parts of the country would find the provisions of the

Friendly Societies Act more suitable to their purposes.

Another special authority is for guaranteeing the performance of their duties by officers of Friendly Societies and branches. Societies for this purpose have been established in connection with some of the large orders with excellent results. Not only are they able to provide the officers of societies with the requisite security on much easier terms than they could get it from an ordinary guarantee company not connected with Friendly Societies, and to relieve them from the invidious position of obtaining the suretyship of personal friends, and their friends from the responsibility, and the societies from the uncertainty of private suretyship; but by means of judicious provisions in the policies they may secure a better audit of the accounts, and may exercise supervision over the financial arrangements of the branches.

A special authority has been granted for playing the game of quoits. In this a liberal interpretation has been placed upon the Act, for while the game in question has doubtless much to recommend it, the pursuit of it is not analogous to the operations of a Friendly Society. It was probably looked upon as akin to a Working-man's Club.

The promotion of literature, science, and the fine arts has also been specially authorized, and might certainly have included the promotion of a knowledge of music, though that is made the subject of a separate special authority. Under this some excellent societies have been able to obtain a legal organization suitable to their wishes, without the expense of registration under the provision of the Companies Act 1867, which enables the word "Limited" to be omitted.

The desire on the part of many branches of Friendly Societies to avoid the loss of interest, which often arises from the difficulty of obtaining investment for small sums, by combining together for the purpose of investment, led to the granting of a special authority for the receipt of the funds of Friendly Societies and branches, and the investment of the same for their benefit. The usefulness of this special authority has now been spent, for the Friendly Societies Act 1895 enabled the object desired to be attained without a separate organization, by simply enacting that one branch might invest its money by the trustees of another branch, of which it formed part. A previous similar enactment was contained in the Act of 1887, but had been found difficult to work on account of the requirement of the consent of the committee or members of the branch whose funds were invested, for each investment. It is now provided that the consent required shall be that only of the committee or members of the branch by which the investment is made. It is presumed, therefore, that this special authority will now fall into disuse and not be renewed. The existing societies registered under it will probably continue their operations, as they have doubtless invested their funds on mortgages and in other ways which it will not be necessary or desirable to call in or realize; but the superior simplicity and safety of the proceeding under the Act will no doubt lead to its being generally adopted, and the specially authorized investment societies being allowed to die out.

An interesting special authority is that granted for enabling persons of the Jewish religion to provide for the due celebration of the Passover, and for the expenses incurred at Passover. That ancient and thrifty race attaches so great a value to the historic observances enjoined by its religion, that among the very poorest of its members the expense of a due celebration of the Passover is contemplated long beforehand, and small sums are set aside, week after week, to accumulate until the time arrives for the sacred festival. In other respects religion and thrift are kept in close connection among the Jewish people. We have seen that the purposes of an ordinary Friendly Society may include for their benefit the observance of "shiva", when the mourner is compelled to abstain from labour for a given time. The societies formed for this purpose usually provide also for conveyances to carry the mourners to the funeral of a member, and for the erection of a tombstone over his remains. It is an object of interest in a Jewish cemetery to observe the number of memorials of the humbler members of the community, bearing the name of the Friendly Society to which they belonged and by which the tombstones were erected. Many of these societies have synagogues of their own, and provide by joint contribution for all the observances of religion, but these are not referred to in the registered rules.

The encouragement and promotion of the riding of bicycles and similar machines may also be the purpose of a registered society.

The promotion of education is an object for which several societies have been formed. Perhaps one of the most curious is a society for the education of political agents in a knowledge of the law relating to corrupt practices.

The promotion of the science and art of cookery will be admitted to be a purpose deserving of every encouragement.

An authority was granted for providing the members with legal and other assistance when claiming compensation under the Employers' Liability Act, but it was pointed out to the societies applying to be registered thereunder, that it was to their own legal advisers that they must look to avoid the perils of champerty and maintenance. The Employers' Liability Acts have been in some degree superseded by the Workmen's Compensation Act 1897, which we propose to consider in a future chapter.

The mutual protection and promotion of the interests of Friendly Societies is a purpose for which another special authority has been obtained. In many parts of the country Friendly Societies combine with great advantage for the discussion of matters that affect their common interests, and for the solution of difficulties that occur in their working, and such combinations enable them to take common action.

Finally, the promotion of the pursuit of angling has been specially authorized. In connection with the gentle craft—the contemplative man's recreation—fishing rights are frequently acquired, and the inexpensive and effectual machinery of the Friendly Societies Act is very useful in simplifying the method of dealing with these rights.

The expression, "Specially Authorized Society", is in some respects an unfortunate one, as it might be taken to imply some particular excellence in the purpose of the society which had induced the Lords of the Treasury to extend to it their special approval. This is curiously the reverse of the fact; for Specially Authorized Societies (with rare exceptions) are refused all the special privileges of a Friendly Society, including the fiscal privilege of exemption from stamp duty. Rather, therefore, than having a claim to special preference, they are placed at a disadvantage. The registry of rules in no case implies any approval of anything they contain; but in the case of a Specially Authorized Society it implies a distinct stamp of inferiority to the other classes of societies which are admitted to the full benefits of the Act.

The latest published returns as to the societies other than Working-men's Clubs, referred to in this chapter, show a capital of £535,301, belonging to 51,068 members in 258 societies.

The reader will probably be surprised to find how multifarious a collection of societies may be brought within the margin of the Friendly Societies Act, and how large a space of man's life may be spent in association under it. In the social intercourse which is to be promoted by the Working-men's Club, in the game of quoits, in the popular and wholesome exercise of bicycle riding, in the contemplative pursuit of angling, in the development of literary, scientific, or artistic tastes, especially in regard to the sublime art of music; in the organization of charity, the promotion of thrift, the relief of the embarrassed by way of loan, the assistance of the unemployed, the promotion of agriculture and horticulture, the promotion of education, especially in that most necessary and specifically human art which is based upon the science of cookery; in association with the religious beliefs of the Hebrew community, as well as in all the ramifications of provident insurance, the Friendly Societies Act is a code of encouragement and a charter of protection.

Chapter VIII.

Old-age Pensions.

We have dwelt upon Friendly Societies mainly in relation to their primary object of assuring sick pay during working life, and have incidentally pointed out the distinctions of various kinds between that assurance and the assurance of old-age pensions or deferred annuities. The question of provision for old age is one, however, that cannot escape the attention of the thoughtful young man in whose position we have sought to place ourselves. He knows that the time must arrive, if he lives, when the cause of inability to work will be, not a casual distemper or accidental injury, but the fact that working days are over. Even in those societies which continue the allowance of sick pay for the whole of life—a plan open to the objections pointed out in chapter VI.—the condition of the allowance is that there shall be some actual sickness, and, however liberally that condition may be interpreted, mere inability to work through old age is not within the terms of the contract. Those terms have been construed by many societies with undue liberality, greatly to the damage and loss of their younger members. Even in those cases where slight evidence of sickness is accepted as sufficient to enable a member to claim sick pay in old age, the allowance granted, which used frequently to be called superannuation, is but small, being usually the quarter pay, viz. 2*s*. 6*d*. or 3*s*. a week. It is not surprising that this disposition towards a liberal construction of the contract should exist, where the member has no other source of maintenance, and would otherwise be compelled to seek relief from the poor-law authorities. A society is naturally unwilling to see its members in old age sink into the condition of paupers, especially where the workhouse test is enforced, and the small allowance which it grants is in general just enough to prevent that calamity. All the evidence seems to show that, though Friendly Societies rarely make direct provision for old age, very few of their members become inmates of a workhouse. It would be so even if the parliamentary returns of paupers who have been members of Friendly Societies were to be trusted; but those returns are in no way to be depended upon, the information they give being neither accurate nor sufficient.

The societies which have thus, by over-generous treatment, protected such of their members against pauperism as would otherwise have fallen into that condition, have done so at the risk of their own stability; and as accurate views are more and more prevailing on the actuarial conditions of financial success in Friendly Societies, it is becoming more and more obvious that the reform of limiting sick pay to a given age will have to be adopted. It was indeed suggested by the Royal Commission on the Aged Poor that the Friendly Societies Act should be altered so that after a certain date members who join a society should be enabled to insure for sick pay up to 65, and for an annuity after that age, but not for sick pay throughout life. The Commissioners hoped that this would have the double effect of securing a regular provision for the old age of Friendly Society members, and averting the danger to the financial stability of the societies caused by the present system of continuous sick pay in old age. It would, as it seems to us, be a complete departure from the present system of freedom of contract in

Friendly Societies, and is to be deprecated upon that ground, if for no other. If the limitation is to extend to registered societies alone, it will encourage the formation of unregistered societies. If it is to extend to both, it cannot be made effectual except by the pernicious system of declaring a contract unenforceable—in the interest only of the rogues who desire to break it. At present the societies appear to be waiting for each other before effecting the reform voluntarily, as the present system is still too attractive to the members for a society rejecting it to meet the competition of those which would still maintain it. When any society or societies shall have adopted a rule limiting sick pay to the age of 65, the problem how to provide for the old age of the members will become a pressing one. The actuarial solution is easy: create a separate pension fund for deferred annuities, commencing at the age of 65, and continuing during the remainder of life; let each member pay into that fund the requisite premium, according to a table of contributions for deferred annuities, and then invest and reinvest until by compound interest the annuities have been made secure.

We have already said that the purchasing a deferred annuity is only one of the many ways of providing for old age. It is undoubtedly an effectual method, but it has never been, and is not likely to become, a popular method. For this there are several reasons. It is costly. Unless begun early in life, the premium necessary to secure a deferred annuity is a heavy tax on wages. It involves the sinking of present money to secure an advantage in the remote future. No man likes to place his savings beyond his control. Its benefits may be small in comparison with the amount paid for them. The member may not live till he is 65, or may live only a short time after. It may absorb savings that would be better applied towards provision for the member's wife and children in the event of his early death.

The objection arising from the uncertainty of life is sometimes proposed to be met by making the premiums returnable in the event of death before attaining the age when the annuity commences, but that can only be done by increasing the amount of the premiums, and thus rendering the transaction more costly. It becomes by this means a mere deposit of savings, and might be carried out with equal or greater advantage by paying the premiums into the Post Office Savings-bank, or otherwise investing them, until the time arrives when the member desires to cease work, and then buying an immediate annuity with the accumulated amount. This plan has the more attraction, that it can be made available if the benefit of it is required before attaining the age of 65; and also that if the member finds himself still able to work at that age, he need not withdraw his accumulations until he wants them, when the provision made by way of pension will be materially increased. The plan of accumulating surplus contributions at interest, and converting them into an immediate annuity when the time arrives, instead of at once applying them to the purchase of a deferred annuity, is that adopted by the societies founded on the model advocated by the late Mr. Holloway, M.P., in his "Forster Prize Essay".

The Aged Poor Commissioners reported that there is undoubtedly a wide-spread dislike of the purchase of deferred annuities, owing largely to a conviction that other forms of thrift are of more value, such as expenditure on the advancement of children, or the application of savings to investment, or in business, so as to yield a permanent return without forfeiture of capital. It is by some of these means, rather than by direct insurance, that members of Friendly Societies have hitherto made provision for old age. If, however, the insurance of sick pay after 65 years of age should be discontinued, a source which has been in fact to a large extent a provision for old age would be dried up, and the necessity of a more general provision by way of deferred annuity would have to be considered. The question would then arise—Have the members of Friendly Societies generally the means of making this provision? Hitherto they have paid inadequate contributions for a partial provision; where will they find the funds for paying adequate contributions for a complete provision? It is alleged by some that the members now pay out of their wages as much as they can afford, and that to call upon them to pay a larger sum towards the future would involve them in present distress. It is alleged by others that it is not so; the extra contribution need not be so large as supposed, and might be brought well within their means. According to the rates charged by the Manchester Unity of Oddfellows, at the age of 21 a weekly contribution of 4⅜*d.* during life would provide 10*s.* sick pay for the first twenty-six weeks of sickness, and 5*s.* afterwards during the whole of life, and funeral benefits; while it would require a weekly contribution of 6⅞*d.*, payable till 65, to assure sick pay up to that age, 5*s.* per week fixed pension after that age, and funeral benefits—the difference being 2½*d.* per week.

It would thus appear that by an additional contribution of 10*s.* 10*d.* per annum beyond the 19*s.* which he now pays, a member of the Manchester Unity at the age of 21 could secure, not merely a fixed pension of £13 a year, but also the cessation of the payment of 19*s.* at the age of 65, equivalent to a pension of £13, 19*s*. a year. Suppose him to be earning 20*s*. a week wages, that is equivalent to increasing his contribution from one week's income per annum to one and a half week's income per annum. There is assuredly nothing in this which places it beyond the range of possibility. We take it for granted that no prudent young man, who applied one week's income per year to pay his friendly society contribution, would fail to set aside in some other form of saving at least another week's income per year. Would he not be doing well to apply half that amount to an absolute provision for old age?

Whence, then, has arisen the cry for state-aided pensions? What young man of 21, having the option presented to him of applying another half-week's pay to this particular object, would say: "This is the last straw that breaks my back; I really cannot afford more than a quarter of a week's pay; I must ask the government to provide me with the other quarter out of the taxes, or the local authorities to provide it out of the rates"? Would he not feel that such an appeal was wholly inconsistent with independence and self-reliance? If the young man of 21 would not say so, why should an older man say so? If he did not in his time purchase a deferred annuity, did he not keep in his pocket the half-week's pay that it would have cost, and invest it in some other equally profitable way? If not, is he not responsible for his own neglect of having done so? What is the foundation of the claim that has been urged on the community at large? Has his income been so small that he could not save one and a half week's of it in the year? Is not this in itself an acknowledgment of improvidence? If it was too small, why did he not take steps to increase it?

The suggestion usually made by the advocates of State-aided Pensions has been that the member should provide himself with half-a-crown a week and the State give another half-crown to make up a total income of 5*s.* a week. According to the rates of the Manchester Unity the weekly contribution at the age of 21 payable till 65 to assure sick pay up to that age, 2*s.* 6*d.* per week fixed pension after that age, and funeral benefits, would be 5¼*d.*, which, as compared with the 4⅜*d.* payable during life for sickness and funeral benefits only, gives a difference of ⅞ths of a penny per week. Thus an additional contribution of 3*s.* 10*d.* beyond the 19*s.* now paid would suffice to secure a fixed pension of £6, 10*s.* a year and the cessation of the payment of 19*s.*, equivalent to a pension of £7, 9*s.* a year. A little more than one day's wages per annum would thus be all that he is called upon to contribute, the State providing the extra 7*s.* per annum. The man who saves one day's wages is to be rewarded by an equivalent of two days' wages from the State, while the man who saves three days' wages is to get nothing. It is not easy to discern any sound principle upon which such an arrangement could be defended.

Others have suggested that every member of a Friendly Society should, when he reaches the age of 65, be granted a free pension of 5*s.* a week by the State. This, at the age of 21, would, according to the Manchester Unity tables, reduce the necessary weekly contribution for sickness and funeral benefits from 4⅜*d.* payable during the whole of life to 3⅝*d.* payable until 65, or from 19*s.* per annum to 15*s.* 9*d.*, less than five days' pay of a man earning 20*s.* per week, and would be equivalent to a State gift to each man of 14*s.* per annum, or more than four days' pay. The employer may be trusted to find this out and reduce the wages accordingly, so that in the long run the gift will be a gift to him and not to the workman, and the State will be endowing out of the general taxation the employer of 1000 workmen with the handsome sum of £700 a year.

Whatever a man's income may be, there seems to be nothing unreasonable in the suggestion that, if he must spend fifty weeks' pay in meeting present necessities, he should at least put aside the other two weeks' pay to provide for future needs. If men framed their standard of living on that principle, they would be able to obtain from their employers wages sufficient to carry it into effect. In all ranks of life there are persons who live up to and even beyond their means, and these persons deserve no sympathy. The man who lives within his means, even to the extent of one-twenty-sixth part, will find that he need ask for none. Certainly the members of Friendly Societies deserve credit for their economy and providence; and equally certainly, the industrial population generally deserve well of the State whom they serve with the strength of their manhood; but it would be a poor acknowledgment of those services to grant them State pensions, which would only tend to lower their wages, and put money in the pockets of their employers.

We wrote in 1890 "that there is no other way of providing for old age than by thrift, self-denial, and forethought in youth"; and the anxious and prolonged consideration we have lately been required to give to the subject, with the most urgent wish to find a favourable solution for its difficulties, has strongly enforced the same lesson. We have not been called upon to consider the proposal that everyone should have a pension.

As it could only be carried into effect by a system of enormous taxation, against which the pension in the case of the wealthy would be a small set-off, it would be nothing but a redistribution of wealth, diminishing the incomes of the wealthy to provide incomes for the poor—a system which might be defensible upon some grounds, but certainly not upon any which have relation to providence, and is therefore quite outside the scope of this work.

Chapter IX.

Workmen's Compensation.

The Workmen's Compensation Act 1897 introduced a new principle into English jurisprudence. Under the Common Law and under the Employers' Liability Act 1880, an employer—like every other person—had been made liable for the consequences of his own acts, and of the acts of those other persons which, upon the principle *qui facit per alium facit per se*, were imputed to him. If I employ the hand of another to do my work, I do the work myself. This principle is somewhat extended by the maxim *respondeat superior.* If my servant in the course of his service injures a third party, it is I, the superior, who must answer for that injury. But how if the person injured is another servant? Here the law interposed a doctrine of "common employment", and excogitated an implied condition in the contract of service that the servant intended to take upon himself the risk that he might be injured by a fellow-servant. The judicature has always felt especial fondness for its own children, and as it is quite certain that this supposed tacit contract never entered the mind of any employer, or of any servant, the judicature has all the rights of paternity in this case. The consequences of this fiction of the law were so intolerable that they were modified, though not entirely removed, by the Act of 1880. Another qualification of employers' liability arose where there had been "contributory negligence" on the part of the person injured. It is my duty so to conduct my business, and to see that my servants so conduct my business, that they do not injure anyone, in obedience to the precept *Sic utere tuo ut alienum non laedas*; but it is equally the duty of other people so to act that they do not needlessly expose themselves to be injured by me or my servants in the lawful conduct of my business, and if they fail in that duty they take the consequences upon themselves. *Vigilantibus, non dormientibus, jura subveniunt.* The law will not look after the interests of those who do not look after their own. The net result of all this is, that if a servant, without neglect or default of his own, is injured by the act or default of his master, or within the limits covered by the Employers' Liability Act 1880, of another servant of his master, the master is liable.

This is still the law: absolutely, as far as regards all occupations to which the Workmen's Compensation Act 1897 does not apply; and it is not repealed as far as regards the occupations to which that Act does apply, but may be put in force at the option of the workman if he prefer it to the remedy which the Act gives him. That remedy is, however, complete. The new Act introduces the principle of insurance—a principle well-known in Germany and other continental countries, but not heretofore applied to the relations of employer and workman in this country. With the exception that the employer is not to be liable where the injury arises from the serious and wilful misconduct of the workman injured, an employer in the industries to which the Act applies is now liable to compensate his workman for any personal injury by accident arising out of and in the course of the employment, whether such injury is or is not caused by any act or default of the employer, or of any servant of his, or of the injured workman himself. The doctrines of common employment and contributory negligence are thus swept out of the way, and it becomes unnecessary to inquire whether anything the employer did or left undone has been the cause of the injury. The employer is required to insure his workmen against accidents of whatever kind occurring out of and in the course of the employment, from any cause other than the serious and wilful misconduct of the injured workman himself.

The insurance so provided differs from ordinary life insurance in being a contract of indemnity. The ordinary contract of life insurance may be of any amount, for which the insurer is willing to pay the corresponding premium; if a company insures my life for £10,000, and I die, it is not open to them to question whether the person entitled to receive the money has suffered any such loss by my death as to require that amount of compensation: the contract is an express contract, and not (like fire insurance or marine insurance) a contract of indemnity. The old doctrine upon which this distinction is founded is that no limit of value can be put upon the life of a man. In the first schedule to the Workmen's Compensation Act 1897 careful provision is made to proportion the compensation to the loss sustained. If death results from the injury, and the deceased leaves a husband, wife, parent, grandparent, step-parent, child, grandchild, or stepchild wholly dependent upon his earnings, a sum not less than £150 nor more than £300, and between those limits equal to his earnings during the last three years of his working life, is to be distributed among such dependants. If he leaves none wholly dependent upon him, but some partially dependent, the £150 may be reduced by agreement or arbitration, to a sum proportionate to the pecuniary loss they have suffered. If he leaves no dependants at all, £10 only is to be allowed, to cover the expenses of medical attendance and burial. If total or partial incapacity for work results from the injury, the workman is to receive a sum measured by the loss of his earnings, not exceeding half his weekly earnings, and not exceeding one pound per week in any case. There is, however, the material qualification that the allowance is not to commence until after the second week of the incapacity.

The Act applies only to employment on, or in, or about a railway, factory, mine, quarry, or engineering work, and to employment on, in, or about any building which exceeds 30 feet in height, and is either being constructed or repaired by means of a scaffolding, or being demolished, and on which machinery driven by steam, water, or other mechanical power is being used for the construction, repair, or demolition thereof. Although many important industries are thus excluded from its operations, those which are included comprise a very large portion of the working population, some of whom are especially exposed to risk of accident. If the Act should be found by experience to work well, it will probably not be difficult to induce the legislature to extend its operations over other industries.

It is evident that this statute materially increases the obligations of employers. The knowledge that workmen have a legal claim to compensation may tend to increase the number of accidents. The assurance companies are asking high rates for insuring employers against their risks under the Act, or rather for reinsuring them. It would become necessary for all insurers who are not possessed of sufficiently large capital to equalize their risks, either to reinsure their risks with some company, or to join with other employers in a mutual scheme of insurance. There will thus arise provident associations of employers.

The Act permits a more satisfactory proceeding. Where employers and workmen are willing to join in a scheme for their mutual benefit, and such scheme can be shown to be, on the whole, not less favourable to the workmen than the Act would be, the employer may contract with any of his workmen that the provisions of the scheme are to be substituted for the provisions of the Act. Where such schemes depend upon a joint contribution of the masters and the men, it has to be shown that the contribution of the master is as great as the payment he would have to make under the Act, and that the benefits the workman is to derive from the master's contributions are equivalent to those he would derive under the Act. For example, where the same benefits as those of the Act are granted, and in addition the first two weeks' inability to labour is provided for, it must be shown that the contribution of the master covers the former, and that of the workmen does not exceed the latter. It is competent, however, for masters and workmen to agree that other benefits shall be substituted for those of the Act, as, for example, a general system of life assurance for the assurance against death by accident, a general system of sick pay for the provision against disablement by accident, or a system of pensions or of medical relief for the benefits of the Act generally. In such case, it has to be shown that the benefits provided out of the employers' contribution are equivalent to those of the Act, and that the workmen's contribution is not more than is necessary to provide the other benefits.

Under the provisions of the statute it will be competent for the employers and workmen to continue (at any rate, with some modification) schemes that have been in beneficial operation for many years. It is not to be supposed that the relations between employers and employed are relations of chronic hostility. They have their diverging interests, as all persons who have dealings together must necessarily have, but they have a common interest, which is often stronger than the tendencies to divergence. Where these common interests lead them to join in arrangements by which the workmen and employers contribute together to a provident fund, the results have been excellent in the establishment of mutual confidence and good feeling between them. This has been shown to a marked extent by unanimous applications on the part of the workmen in certain industries for certificates to schemes in which the benefits provided have been shown upon inquiry not to be equal to those of the Act, and the contribution of the employers not to be equal to that of the workmen. They have felt that the indirect advantages of maintaining the existing amicable relations and avoiding litigation were so great that they would have been glad to continue the existing provisions and waive the advantages they might derive from the Act. This is obviously not practicable, and when the necessity of increasing their contributions to the joint fund has been pointed out to the employers, it has been cheerfully accepted—a circumstance which leads to the hope and confident expectation that the provision for contracting out may tend greatly to promote industrial peace and welfare.

The conditions under which contracting out of the Act is permitted are the following:—

1. The Registrar must take steps to ascertain the views of the employer and workmen. This is a condition precedent, and no certificate can be granted to a scheme until it has been fulfilled. For this purpose, the Registrar requires that formal application for a certificate should be made by the employer and by some of the workmen on behalf of as many as agree in the application, setting forth the nature of the scheme, and the views (*a*) of the employer, (*b*) of the workmen, as to its operation. Where the workmen who join in the application are not the whole body of the workmen in the employment, he requests that copies of the scheme may be printed, and hung up in every workshop, and appoints a time within which the dissentient workmen may address communications to him, stating their views. This appears to be required by the Act, although as no scheme can be certified which contains an obligation upon the workmen to join it as a condition of their hiring, the dissentient workmen are not bound by the scheme. It has the advantage, if acted upon, of enabling the Registrar to hear both sides of the question, and possibly to suggest some modification of the scheme which would enable the dissentient workmen to take advantage of it. As we have seen, the mere consent of a certain number, or even of all of the workmen, in a given employment is not of itself sufficient to show that a scheme is on

the whole not less favourable to them than the provisions of the Act would be.

2. The Registrar must certify that the scheme is on the whole not less favourable to the general body of workmen and their dependants than the provisions of the Act. The consent of the workmen not being conclusive, it must be found as a fact that it is not less favourable to them than the Act would be. In order to arrive at a judgment upon this point, many things have to be considered. One of great importance is, the previous experience of accidents in the industry. There is no general scale of liability to accident which can be applied without discrimination to any industry. Even in the same calling, as, for instance, the mining industry, the liability to accident differs in different districts, and is greater or less according to the nature of the mine, the method of working, the customs of the miners, the efficiency of the control and regulation, and other circumstances. The best plan appears to be to take the experience of the particular workmen affected during as long a series of years as it can be conveniently supplied, and apply to it the provisions of the Act, so as to ensure that the employer shall pay in future years at least as much as he would have had to pay in past years if the Act had then been in force. The past is not conclusive as to the future; for the experience of the past few years may have been favourable, and it may be right to allow a margin for the probability that that of the next few years may exceed the average. Something also may have to be allowed for defects in the record. Again, the Act itself, by the greater liberality of its provisions, may tend to increase the

> number and the prolongation of the claims, but this latter is a risk which some might think ought in equity to be borne by the workmen.

The next question to be considered, is whether the workmen will derive an equivalent advantage under the scheme to that which they derive under the Act. To solve it, it is necessary to see in what respects the assurance against accident provided by the scheme is less than that provided by the Act, and what are the other benefits which the scheme provides corresponding to the difference. A form commonly taken by schemes is that of joint equal contribution and joint management between the employer and the workmen. Where this is the case, it will follow that the aggregate benefits the workman is to derive under the scheme must be at least double the aggregate benefits the workman would derive under the Act if there were no scheme. It will be observed that it is not necessary to show that each individual workman will get twice as much as the Act would give him, but only that the advantages to the general body of workmen are on the whole not less. The discretion left to the Registrar is so absolute and so uncontrolled that it would be open to him to take any surrounding circumstance into consideration, but it will probably be wise for him in general to restrict himself to the question of actual financial equivalents.

It will appear from what has been said that the expression in the rubric of the Act which describes these schemes as "contracting-out" schemes is hardly accurate. When it is made essential to such a scheme that the workmen shall have that which an independent officer declares to be an equivalent for all that the Act would give them, the scheme becomes rather a means of carrying the Act into effect than a means of contracting-out of it. Either by schedule or by scheme the workman is to get in meal or in malt all that the Act says he shall have.

Having regard to the difficulty of ascertaining with precision what is an exact equivalent to the benefits provided by the Act, two important safeguards are contained in it. The Registrar may give a certificate to expire at the end of a limited period not less than five years; and it is proposed that that period should in general be five years and six months, so as to allow of a quinquennial actuarial valuation being made, and thus of any defect in the original scheme being ascertained and remedied before the certificate is renewed. The Registrar may also revoke the certificate upon complaint made by or on behalf of the workmen. It is to be observed that the certificate is not to be revoked at the instance of the employer, who is held to his bargain as long as the certificate remains in force, even though the scheme should be shown by experience to be more burdensome on him than the Act would have been. The complaint of the workmen may be on any of the following grounds:—

1. That the provisions of the scheme are no longer so favourable to the general body of workmen and their dependants as the provisions of the Act.
2. That the provisions of the scheme are being violated.
3. That the scheme is not being fairly administered.
4. That satisfactory reasons exist for revoking the certificate.

Upon receiving such a complaint, the Registrar is to examine into it. If satisfied that good cause exists for it, he is to give an opportunity to the employer to remove the cause of complaint. If this is not done, the Registrar has no option in the matter, but is required by the Act to revoke the certificate. Upon the revocation of a certificate, or if one expires and is not renewed, the funds held for the purpose of the scheme are to be distributed as the employer and workmen agree, or if they fail to agree, as the Registrar may determine.

When a scheme has been certified, the Registrar may require the employer to answer inquiries and to furnish accounts in regard to it; and thus information may gradually be accumulated which will in time change the present experimental and provisional character of the measure into one of more assured certainty. Looking at the statute as a whole, whether its provisions are carried out in their integrity, or are substituted by an equivalent certified scheme, we anticipate that it will be beneficial. It had long been admitted on all sides that the Employers' Liability Act of 1880 required amendment, and that cases of great hardship arose under it. The further modification or entire repeal of the doctrine of common employment had frequently been proposed; but the present statute takes the wiser and more comprehensive course of rendering it immaterial, so far as the purview of the Act extends. As we have said, it imposes a new burden on the employer; and the bill met with criticism upon that ground; but it must be borne in mind that it is really beyond the power of the legislature permanently to disturb the relations between master and workman. If the existing wages paid to the workmen are adequate, and this Act transfers from the shoulders of the workmen to those of the employer the burden, whatever it may be, of insurance against accidents for which the employer was not liable when that rate of wages was settled, the burden will only rest there until the next occasion when the rate of wages comes up for settlement, when it will be shifted back again to the shoulders of the workmen in the form of a diminution of wages. If the existing wages paid to the workmen are not adequate, the transfer to the employer of that burden merely anticipates an increase of those wages which would have had to be granted in due course. It is the market, not the legislature, that can alone determine what a workman's wages shall be. The temporary incidence of this extra burden on the employer has undoubtedly raised a temporary sense of grievance. In like manner, among the workmen, the long-standing conviction that contracting-out would place them at a disadvantage, and that they did not meet the employer on equal terms when they retired from the strong position given to them by the Act, has led them in some branches of industry to look with coldness upon proposals for mutual schemes: but this feeling will probably give way when it is found by experience that what are called contracting-out schemes are not really so. Under the schedule of the Act, the workmen obtain a substantial advantage, the benefits of which they will reap until some future reduction in wages takes place, and the individual workman gets a protection against the casualties attending his industry which he had not before. Under the equivalent schemes, encouragement is given to the establishment and maintenance of good feeling between employers and workmen, and to their forming and manifesting a common interest in the better providing not alone against casual risks but against the ordinary and certain ills of life.

Chapter X.

Co-operative Societies.

Having provided the young man whom we have conjectured at the beginning of several previous chapters with insurance against a great many contingencies, we will now imagine him, a little later on in life, happily married, but finding that his income, after payment of his Friendly Society contributions, does not go far in procuring for his wife and little family the necessaries, not to say the comforts, he would like them to enjoy. He will be shrewd enough to see that for many things which he has to buy in small quantities, he pays a much higher relative price than the rich man, who can afford to buy the same things in large quantities. He will observe, moreover, that tradesmen give credit to others, if they will not to himself, and frequently make bad debts; and he knows that those who do pay must necessarily make up for those who do not. He concludes that, for this reason also, he is paying for what he buys more than its real value. If he himself obtains credit from the tradesmen, he finds himself even worse off, for he knows he must pay some day, and in the meanwhile has to accept what quality of goods his creditor may impose upon him. Finally, he has no substantial guarantee for the purity of the things that are supplied. Here the co-operative store comes to his assistance. A combination of small retail buyers can go into the market, get what its members want at wholesale prices, and either distribute it among them at cost price, or return the overplus to them as profit; it gives, or ought to give, no credit, at any rate none beyond what each member has deposited in the fund as his share money; and it has no temptation to buy and distribute impure commodities, but, on the contrary, makes it a principle to obtain a guarantee of purity. This is the distributive department of its working. The power of combination goes much further. The distributive store dispenses with one of the middlemen who do so much to increase the price of commodities—the retail dealer; but it has to go to the wholesale dealer, who is another middleman. If a co-operative store, or a union of a number of co-operative stores, produce the goods themselves, they may dispense with him. Thus we get productive co-operation.

Mr. Holyoake, the historian of co-operation, tells (in a charming book entitled *Self-help One Hundred Years Ago*, published in 1888) the story of the establishment, by Dr. Shute Barrington, Bishop of Durham, in the year 1794, of a co-operative store at Mongewell, in Oxfordshire, for the benefit of the poor of that and three small adjoining parishes. The bishop thus describes its operations: "A quantity of such articles of consumption as they use was procured from the wholesale dealers, as bacon, cheese, candles, soap, and salt, to be sold at prime cost, and for ready money. They were restricted in their purchases to the supposed weekly demand of their families. The bacon and cheese, being purchased in Gloucestershire, had the charge of carriage." The storekeeper was an infirm old man, unable to read or write, but so correct in his receipts that there was no reason to regret his want of scholarship. "As he had parish pay, and his house rent was discharged, he was perfectly contented with his salary of one shilling per week, having also the common benefit of the shop." The transactions in 1796 amounted to £223, 14*s.* 2*d.*, and produced a saving of £48, 1*s*., or 21 per cent. From the adoption of this plan, the bishop observes, "the poor will have good weight, and articles of the best quality; which, without imputing dishonesty to the country shopkeeper, will not always be the case at a common shop. . . . Another benefit of this measure is the preventing the poor running into debt. The credit given them adds much to the sufferings they undergo from their situation. . . . Another striking benefit to be derived is giving to the poor the full enjoyment of their earnings; for whoever attends to the circumstances under which the labouring country poor usually purchase the necessaries of life must be sensible of the inconveniences to which they are subjected." Mr. Holyoake mentions also two other stores established shortly afterwards:—one by the Rev. Dr. Glasse at Greenford, and the other by the Rev. George Glasse at Hanwell, both in Middlesex, which were opened in 1800.

The oldest productive co-operative institution was the Hull Anti-Mill and General Industrial Society, established in 1795, and registered in 1856. It existed more than 100 years, and was wound up in 1897.

Mr. Holyoake mentions, as next in order, a parish windmill erected in 1796 on Barham Downs. Eight subscribers furnished a capital of £40 each to start it, and the profits, after paying them interest at 5 per cent, were to be applied towards reducing the capital to £150, and afterwards to the benefit of the labouring industrious poor of the parish. A similar mill was erected in 1797 at Chislehurst in Kent.

Two existing co-operative societies date back to the year 1800. The Bridgeton Old Victualling and Baking Society in the county of Lanark has 1056 members, and carries on a business of £66,944 a year on a capital of

£3230. It showed a balance of profit on the year's transactions of £15,251, and has assets worth £11,548. The Pelican Provident Society at Radford, Notts, has only 33 members, and its receipts and expenditure were both £605.

Nineteen other existing societies, 10 in England and 9 in Scotland, began before the Victorian era. The Lennoxtown Friendly Victualling Society, Stirlingshire (1812), is distributive, and turns over £160 a week. The Sheerness Economical Industrial and Provident Society, Kent (1816), has 1334 members, and does a business of £28,569 a year. Its capital is £17,272, and its assets £20,092. The Larkhall Victualling Society, Lanark (1821), does £20,708 a year. The Meltham Mills Provident Co-operative Trading Society, Yorkshire (1827), £4628. The Leven Baking Society, Fifeshire (1828), £7410. The Upperby Industrial Society, Cumberland (1829), £2878. The Paddock Friendly Co-operative Trading Society, Yorkshire (1830), £4072. The Bannockburn Co-operative Society, Stirling (1830), £30,699. Its capital is £12,518, and its assets £17,236, of which £6052 is buildings, fixtures, and land used in trade. The Parkhead and Westmuir Economical Society, Glasgow (1831), sells for £17,571, and has £10,617 assets, of which £6424 is buildings, &c.

Five existing societies date from the year 1832. The Stockport Great Moor Society turns over £7431 a year. Two societies at Foleshill, the Lockhurst Lane Society, £11,038, and the Stoney Stanton Road Prudential Society, £10,947. The Ripponden Society, £10,635. The Cadder Society, Lanark, £11,141.

The Arbroath Equitable Society, having 1061 members and £10,146 capital, does £18,989 business, and has £14,076 assets. The Brechin United Co-operative Association, with 1100 members and £12,800 capital, does £35,050 a year, and its assets are £34,210. Both these Forfarshire societies were established in 1833.

The Arbroath West Port Association, in the same county, was established in 1834. It has 2229 members, whose investments amount to £24,148. It turns over £49,142 a year, and has £32,834 assets. The Field Head Society, at Kirkheaton, established in the same year, does £5882 business.

Whether the Devonport Coal Association, established in 1837, is to be treated as before or after the accession of Her Majesty, does not appear, but it has ever since continued its modest but useful operations, and supplies its 842 members with coal to the value of £2381 a year.

The co-operative enterprises of Robert Owen, dictated by a comprehensive spirit of philanthropy, do not appear in England even to have lasted for his lifetime. Those founded by him in America did not for a long period survive him.

A great impetus was given to the co-operative movement by the efforts of the brilliant group of young men who were the friends and disciples of the Rev. Frederick Denison Maurice, and though the particular institutions founded by them had a comparatively brief existence, the influence of their advocacy and energy has never spent itself. Of all the names which deserve to be venerated by co-operators, that of Mr. Edward Vansittart Neale stands foremost. A country squire and large land-owner, he sacrificed much of his wealth for the benefit of the labouring poor. When these munificent gifts were exhausted, he might have been pardoned if he had thought that he had done enough, and even if he had turned with some bitterness from the scene of failure and of ingratitude. That was not his nature. He remained during the whole of a long life the trusted friend and adviser of the co-operative movement, and late in years, when the office of secretary to the Co-operative Union was vacant, the grand old man, who had succeeded to a beautiful landed estate on the banks of the Thames, accepted the arduous office without fee or reward, and laboured at its routine duties, constantly travelling from London to Manchester, till almost the close of his life. He was a skilful conveyancer, and aided the societies by his legal knowledge and ingenuity to surmount many difficulties.

Among the same group were the Rev. Charles Kingsley, whose forcible writings under the name of "Parson Lot" did much to awaken public feeling on the evils which made the hearts of these "Christian Socialists" burn within them, and whose career is traced by the sympathetic pen of Dean Stubbs in another volume of the present series; Mr. Thomas Hughes, afterwards member of Parliament, Queen's Counsel, and judge of County Courts, and his close friend Mr. John Malcolm Ludlow, of whom we have already said something in chapter I., and who is now the last survivor. These also were the lifelong friends and advisers of the co-operative movement, which they benefited by their legal skill and knowledge, as well as by their eloquent pens and voices, their far-seeing judgment, their strong convictions, and their invincible uprightness and sincerity.

An even more powerful impetus was given to the movement by the remarkable success which attended some of the stores in Lancashire. In 1844, a few working men of Rochdale joined in establishing the Equitable Pioneer Society, and that society extended its operations so rapidly, and conferred such signal benefits upon its members, that its prosperity led to the establishment of other similar societies in many parts of the country. It thus vindicated its title of "pioneers", for in its constitution and rules it embodied all the best principles, the generous and progressive ideas, which have characterized the movement. It now has 12,719 members, with a capital of £360,371. Its sales during the year 1896 were £292,336, and its profits £36,552, of which it applied £892 to educational purposes. The total assets are £384,467. While so many other societies have succumbed to the temptation of giving credit, this pioneer society has remained true to its original co-operative principles, and still gives no credit.

Some statistics illustrating the rapid growth of co-operative societies are given in the *Wholesale Societies Annual.* In 1862 the total sales of the societies are recorded as £2,333,523; by 1872 they had increased to £13,012,120; by 1882 to £27,541,212; and in 1895 they were £55,100,249, or nearly 24 times the figure of 1862. On the 31st December, 1895, their members numbered 1,430,340, having a share capital of £16,749,826, and a loan capital of £4,581,573. The profits for the year were £5,389,071. The total sales from 1862 to 1895 are summed up as £815,760,341, and the total profits during the same time as £72,075,568.

Other statistics, which have recently been published by a committee of the International Co-operative Congress, enable us to distinguish between the various classes of co-operative societies. They state the number of distributive societies or stores as 1453, and the number of wholly productive societies as 259. Exclusive of credit banks, the total number of co-operative societies is given as 1741. It will of course be understood that many of the societies reckoned as distributive, that being their main function, have important productive departments. The number of members in distributive societies is for England 1,142,204, for Scotland 233,907, for Ireland 1925; in productive societies 25,637, and in all societies except credit banks 1,492,371. The number of persons employed by the productive societies is 8475; and the total number of persons employed by all the societies is 61,322, of which 33,619 are engaged in the productive departments of work.

The sales of the Distributive Societies in England were £29,342,755, in Scotland £7,547,397, in Ireland £51,878; of the Productive Societies, £2,625,938; of all the societies, £57,318,426. These figures sufficiently indicate the great expansion of the co-operative movement since the commencement of the Victoria era.

The Friendly Societies Act of 1846 enabled societies to be established for the frugal investment of the savings of the members by providing themselves with corn, coal, flour, and other necessaries, and under this Act the Rochdale Pioneers and many other early societies were registered. The legal advisers of the societies, notably Mr. Ludlow and Mr. Neale, drew attention to some provisions of the Friendly Societies Acts then in force which hampered their operations, and Mr. H. A. Slaney, at their instance, introduced a Bill which became the Industrial and Provident Societies Act 1852. This Act, though it opened a separate register for these societies, continued to apply to them many of the clauses of the Friendly Societies Act. The expression, "Industrial and Provident Societies", which it introduced, has never superseded the term "Co-operative Societies", by which they are familiarly known. It aptly indicates their two-fold operation. They are "industrial" in their productive sense, as combining the labour of many for the benefit of the whole; they are "provident" in the distributive sense, as enabling the member to economize the cost of the necessaries of life, and thus to obtain some modest luxuries, to increase his standard of comfort, to accumulate profits, to apply them to educational purposes, to become by their means the proprietor of his own dwelling, and in many other ways to improve his position. The industrial side of the system is most truly co-operative when it pays good wages, and gives the worker a share in the profits.

By 1862 the growth and development of the system rendered further legislation necessary, and a new act was passed, granting the societies the privilege of incorporation, and assimilating them rather to companies under the Companies Acts than to societies under the Friendly Societies Act. It retained, however, their more cheap and simple system of registration. They became, in fact, what the French call *sociétés à capital variable*, and in that lay the principal distinction between them and companies with fixed capital.

In 1867 further amendments were made.

In 1876 Mr. Neale prepared a bill to consolidate and amend the acts relating to Industrial and Provident Societies, which was passed in August of that year. The tendency apparent in 1862 and 1867 to assimilate the law to that of Companies was now completely reversed, for with the exception of the incident of incorporation and its consequences, the Act is almost a transcript of the Friendly Societies Act of the previous year.

In 1893 the Co-operative Union, with the aid of Mr. George Howell, M.P., obtained the passing of another consolidating and amending act. The amendments it introduced were few, but some of them were important. The Act of 1876 had provided for the free inspection of the books by every member or person having an interest in the funds, saving only such entries as related to the individual affairs of other members. The Act of 1893 materially restricts this right, except in the case where it is granted by a subsequent amendment of rules.

The Act enables societies to receive deposits of 10 shillings at one time instead of 5 shillings, and it reduces the number of members who may apply to the registrar to appoint inspectors or call a special meeting to one-tenth of the whole number, or where the whole number exceeds 1000, to 100 members. Among the privileges which the legislature grants to the societies are exemption from income-tax, where the society is not one that is limited to a certain number of members, and that deals with the public; nomination for payments at death; and all the privileges of incorporation.

The important development of Co-operative Societies into a kind of co-operation raised to the second power, or co-operation among the societies by the combination of the local stores as corporate shareholders into a wholesale society, for supplying them with the commodities they sell by retail, occurred in 1864 in England and in 1868 in Scotland. The progress of both societies has been very rapid. In 1865 the sales of the English Wholesale were £120,754; in 1880, £3,339,681; in 1896, £11,115,056. It consists of 1044 societies, which have in the whole 993,564 members, and have subscribed a capital of £682,656. It acts as their banker, and turns over in that capacity forty millions sterling per annum, holding in loans and deposits £1,195,895. It runs 7 steamships, and employs 8647 persons, of whom 5214 are in the productive works. Its profits for the year were £177,419, and its total profits from the beginning, £1,842,722, upon total sales amounting to £135,769,821, which may indicate how near it is able to approach the supply of goods at cost price. The Scottish Wholesale Society sold in 1869 for £81,094; in 1880, for £845,221; and in 1896, for £3,822,580, showing progress somewhat less rapid than that of the English Wholesale, but still very great.

A further development of the movement took place in 1869, when the first Co-operative Congress was opened by an address from Mr. Thomas Hughes. He referred to a previous Co-operative Conference that had been held in 1852, in the hall belonging to the Working Tailors' Association of that day. That association, which gave so much innocent pride to Charles Kingsley, when he first put on the coat it had made for him, was broken up, and of the fifteen working associations, as distinguished from co-operative stores, which had been represented at that conference, only one, the Hatters' Association of Manchester, had survived to 1869. At that time, therefore, productive associations were a failure, but the co-operative stores, and their centre, the Wholesale, which was then called the North of England Co-operative Wholesale Society, were prosperous and progressive. They had, indeed, arrived at a point when they no longer required some of the capital which their members had subscribed, and part of Mr. Hughes's address was directed towards advising them not to return their excess of capital, but to use it in the encouragement of productive undertakings.

Of recent years, the productive movement, as may have been gathered from the statistics we have already given, has much increased. In one branch of productive industry, co-operative farming, many attempts have been made, but have not in general been permanently successful. A recent development of co-operation is the establishment in Ireland of a number of co-operative creameries, which give promise of excellent results; and another is the establishment of agricultural credit banks. To credit societies registered under the Friendly Societies Act as specially authorized societies we have referred in a previous chapter. As to those registered under the Industrial and Provident Societies Act, the requirement that the capital is to be divided into shares, and the privilege of limitation of liability, are inconsistent with the adoption in its integrity of the Raiffeisen system. Societies to carry on the business of banking generally have also been registered, but some of them are of doubtful stability.

The legislative definition of the purposes for which Industrial and Provident Societies may be registered has passed through some suggestive changes. In 1862 it was "for carrying on any labour, trade, or handicraft, including the business of banking, and applying the profits to any purposes mentioned in the Rules". In 1871 the trade of the buying and selling of land was defined as a trade that might be carried on. In 1876 the words as to profits were omitted. In 1893 the definition was altered to "any industry, trade, or business, including dealings of any description with land". This is comprehensive enough to permit of almost any society being registered under the Act. Working-men's clubs, "to carry on the business of club proprietors", and a host of miscellaneous bodies have thus been incorporated. The fact of registry under the Act is not therefore conclusive evidence that a society is genuinely co-operative.

Since the Act of 1871 was passed, many Industrial

and Provident Land and Building Societies have been formed. They differ from societies under the Building Societies Acts, to which we shall refer in a future chapter, in respect that the interest of a member in an Industrial and Provident Society is limited by the Statute to £200. They have therefore been mostly concerned in the allotment and distribution of small estates. There has also for many years been growing up in the co-operative stores a movement for applying their profits and accumulated funds towards enabling the members to buy their own houses. We drew the attention of the Statistical Society to this movement in 1876, when we showed that in 1872 about a quarter of a million had been so employed. By 1891 this had increased to £2,497,855. About one-half of this has been accumulated by societies in Lancashire, one-fourth in Yorkshire, and one-fourth in the remainder of the United Kingdom.

From the earliest formation of co-operative stores, it has been made a feature of the scheme that some of the profits should be applied to educational purposes. This is a matter that should not be overlooked, even in so brief a summary of the subject as the present, because it embodies the idea of self-improvement and self-help, which is fundamental to the movement. The general practice is to apply a specific small proportion of the profits to an educational fund, and entrust the application of the money to a sub-committee. In this way many fine libraries have been formed and reading-rooms opened, and other educational measures adopted. An act passed in the session of 1898 has for object the enabling the committees of these and other libraries to regulate and maintain order in them. The Co-operative Wholesale Societies have developed the educational branch of their work by the publication in their annual reports of a series of instructive articles by writers of authority upon economic subjects.

A report presented to the Co-operative Congress of 1898 by its special committee on education, divides the educational work of the movement into three branches: education in the principles and methods of co-operation, provision for the acquisition of knowledge on general subjects, and arrangements for recreation and pleasure. Upon these, as much as £42,391 was expended in the year 1895. The committee made a number of practical recommendations, with a view to promote the study of economic theory and practice and of citizenship, and to act in conjunction with local bodies in the furtherance of technical education. From the very first the education of the citizen has been the aim of co-operators, and it is rather in such moral aims than in any specialization of method that the idea of true co-operation consists. In this connection, it is interesting to note that the co-operators have commemorated the labours of Judge Hughes and Mr. Neale by the foundation of scholarships at Oriel College, Oxford; and that university extension lectures and classes for study, and examinations with rewards to successful students under the auspices of the Co-operative Union, are largely supported by them.

However some of the more enthusiastic spirits, who saw in the co-operative movement the promise of a coming millennium, may have been disappointed, its beneficial operation in contributing to the material comfort and the mental progress of the members has been immeasurable. Like all spontaneous and self-regulating processes, it has given rise to varieties of treatment and differences of opinion among its ardent promoters. These have had relation, in many cases, to the burning question, how to apply the profits; a question which is in a large degree the test of the really co-operative character of a society. Like all trading operations, it has had its periods of depression, and the managers and members have been taught some hard lessons in the school of experience, as may be inferred from the fact that the mean expectation of future existence of a co-operative society at the date of its formation has been ascertained by calculation to be about thirteen years; but the spirit of self-reliance, which first inspired it, has enabled them speedily to recover lost ground, and the co-operative movement stands to-day as one of the most practical and the most successful efforts to promote industrial welfare.

Its beneficial operation has extended far beyond the range of the actual members of societies. The competition which it has set up with the local tradesmen has shown them that it is as unwise as it is unfair to make the purchaser who pays cash provide for the loss of interest and sometimes of principal caused by the purchaser who takes credit, and has reduced the share of the middleman in the profit of commodities to a minimum. The whole community has benefited by this change.

The example shown by the Rochdale pioneers has had its direct followers among other classes of persons. The Civil Service Supply Association is a registered Industrial and Provident Society. Other large stores have been constituted under the Companies Acts, such as the Civil Service Co-operative Society, the Army and Navy Co-operative Society, the Army and Navy Auxiliary Society, and the Junior Army and Navy Co-operative Society. The curious observer at the doors of any of those institutions may find food for reflection in the thought that the same means by which the necessaries of life have been cheapened and improved for the poor have been found available to increase the luxuries and amenities of life for the rich.

Chapter XI.

Building Societies.

Our thoughtful and prosperous young working-man will find that house rent forms a considerable portion of his expenditure, and will set himself to devise some means by which that burden can be diminished. He will reflect that the good and paying tenant has to make up to the landlord the losses he sustains from tenants who cannot and tenants who will not pay; that it is bothersome to have to go to the landlord for every necessary repair and every desirable improvement to the premises; that if he were the owner of his own house he could contrive many convenient and useful fixtures that it would be folly for him to make while the landlord has the power to appropriate them to himself on the determination of the tenancy, or possibly to make them the subject of a claim for increase of rent. The more he gets accustomed to the house which has been the scene to himself and his wife of so many innocent pleasures and home endearments, the more he will wish to make it his own. We have seen to how large an extent this instinct has been satisfied by appropriations of the accumulated funds of Co-operative Societies. A similar movement has been taking place for some years in Friendly Societies, especially where there are District Investment funds, to which the subordinate branches contribute. It becomes essential to lay such funds out to the best advantage, and a long mortgage on a freehold or leasehold house, repayable by instalments, produces as large a return of interest as any sound security can give with little pressure upon the borrower. The objection that would be felt to locking up the money for a long time by the individual lodge or court, viz., that the money might be wanted to meet the claims upon the fund before the end of the term, is not great where a central fund is formed by the contributions of many lodges or courts, inasmuch as all are not likely to be wanting their money at the same time, and the accruing income from repayments and interest will in general be sufficient to meet the claims as they accrue. Hence a very considerable business, in the nature of a Building Society business, has come to be transacted as a means of the investment of the funds of Friendly Societies.

Building Societies, strangely so called, for they never build, but are societies for lending money on mortgage to their members, were first specifically dealt with by the legislature in 1836, the last year of the reign of King William IV. Their existence as bodies specially encouraged and protected by the law is exactly commensurate with the Victorian era. The Act 6 and 7 William IV. cap. 32, enacted that all Building Societies established prior to the 1st June, 1836, should be entitled to its benefits on their then present rules being duly certified by the Barrister and deposited with the Clerk of the Peace as directed by the Friendly Societies Acts, without altering in any manner the rules under which they were governed. The preamble alleged that societies, commonly called Building Societies, had been established in different parts of the kingdom, principally amongst the industrious classes, for the purpose of raising by small periodical subscriptions a fund to assist the members thereof in obtaining a small freehold or leasehold property. A mention of "Building Clubs" in Birmingham occurs in 1795; one is known to have been established by deed in 1809 at Greenwich; another is said to have been founded in 1815 under the auspices of the Earl of Selkirk at Kirkcudbright. Other institutions of a similar kind were afterwards established in Scotland under the title of "Menages", and the system was soon adopted by societies formed in the neighbourhood of Manchester and Liverpool and other parts of the North of England. Though the expression "Building Society" was commonly used, yet in London and other parts some further descriptive title was frequently added, such as "Accumulating Fund", "Savings Fund", or "Investment Association". Several societies were described as "Societies for obtaining freehold property", or as "Mutual Associations", or "Societies of Equality". In Scotland, the expression "Property Investment Company" was frequently used. After the passing of the Act in 1836 the expression "Benefit Building Society" became general, and from 1849 to 1874 was the one solely adopted.

The Act of 1874 divided Building Societies into two classes:—a terminating society being one which by its rules is to terminate at a fixed date, or when a result specified in its rules is attained; a permanent society, one which has not by its rules any such fixed date or specified result at which it shall terminate. Permanent societies were not invented until 1846. The early societies were all terminating, consisting of a limited number of members, and coming to an end as soon as every member had received the amount agreed upon as the value of his shares. We borrow from our own article in the ninth edition of the *Encyclopædia Britannica* a simple typical example of the working of such a society. The shares are £120 each, realizable by subscription of 10*s*. a month during 14 years. Fourteen years happens to be nearly the time in which, at 5 per cent compound interest, a sum of money becomes doubled. Hence, the present value, at the commencement of the Society, of the £120 to be realized at its conclusion, or (what is the same thing) of the subscription of 10*s*. a month by which that £120 is to be raised, is £60. If such a society had issued £120 shares, the aggregate subscriptions for the first month of its existence would amount to exactly the sum required to pay the member the present value of one share. One member would accordingly receive a sum down of £60; and in order to protect the other members from loss, would execute a mortgage of his dwelling-house for ensuring the payment of the future subscriptions of 10*s*. per month until every member had in like manner obtained an advance upon his shares, or accumulated the £120 per share. As £60 is not of itself enough to buy a house, even of the most modest kind, every member desirous of using the Society for its expressed purpose of obtaining a dwelling-house by its means would require to take more than one share. This and other causes would give rise to delay and consequent loss of interest; and the question soon arose whether it would not be advantageous to the Society to borrow money in aid of the subscriptions of the members for obtaining advances more speedily.

The definition of Building Societies in the Act of 1836 was in many respects perplexing. "Societies for the purpose of raising, by the monthly or other subscriptions of the several members of such societies, shares not exceeding the value of £150 for each share, such subscription not to exceed in the whole *20s.* per month for each share, a stock or fund for the purpose of enabling each member thereof to receive out of the funds of such society the amount or value of his or her share or shares therein, to erect or purchase one or more dwelling-house or dwelling-houses, or other real or leasehold estate, to be secured by way of mortgage to such society until the amount or value of his or her shares shall have been fully repaid to such society with the interest thereon, and all fines or other payments incurred in respect thereof." The limitations of shares parenthetically introduced were probably intended to confine the operations of the society to the "industrious" classes, but as the limitations attached only to shares, and there was nothing to prevent a single member holding any number of shares, they were of no effect. The words relating to erection or purchase of houses and estates might also have been intended as restrictive, but it was judicially decided that they did not prevent a member obtaining an advance on property already in his possession. The question whether the Act admitted of a society borrowing money passed through several different phases. At first rules were made by several societies authorizing it, and some such rules are to this day acted upon without restriction as to amount. After a while, doubts were raised, and the Attorney-General of the day was appealed to. He gave it as his opinion that no rule for borrowing could be certified as in conformity with law and with the provisions of the Acts. This opinion was acted upon for some years, until the validity of a rule for borrowing came for judicial decision before Vice-Chancellor Page Wood, afterwards Lord Hatherley, who held that the rule was good, provided it was limited to such reasonable amount or proportion of the advances as would secure that the borrowing was for the legitimate purposes of the society.

As time went on, the Act of 1836 was found to be defective in many other respects. It applied to Building Societies all the provisions of the Friendly Societies Acts of 1828 and 1834, so far as the same or any part thereof may be applicable to the purpose of any Benefit Building Society, and to the framing, certifying, enrolling and altering the rules thereof. A few years after, those Acts were repealed as regards Friendly Societies, but being thus incorporated in the Building Societies Act, their obsolete provisions remained still applicable as regards Benefit Building Societies. They left in doubt the question whether a person under age could be a member. He could of course be a member of a Friendly Society, but as he could not execute a mortgage or erect or purchase a house, could he be a member of a Building Society? As the Building Society movement grew, it was found that, in addition to their original object, Building Societies were very useful and remunerative means of investment; and as an encouragement to thrift, many parents desired to induce their children to become members of Building Societies in early life, and it was doubtful whether they could lawfully do so. Gradually, the members of Building Societies separated into two distinct classes, borrowing members and investing members; but the Act of 1836 seems to have contemplated that every member (except, at any rate, the last) should be a borrowing member. As under the Acts of 1828 and 1834 all documents relating to a Building Society had to be enrolled with the Clerk of the Peace for the county in which it was established, it could not remove its place ot meeting out of that county; thus, a society established on the south side of the Thames could not remove to the north side, nor a society in Birkenhead change its place of meeting to Liverpool. These Acts contained no provisions enabling a society to change its name; and greatly restricted societies in the investment of their surplus funds.

The development of the system of Permanent Societies brought these and other defects of the law into prominence. The terminating form of society works smoothly in its earlier years, but as the society approaches its termination, difficulties arise in obtaining interest for its money on account of the shortness of the term for which an advance can be made. Hence arose a practice of establishing a series of societies in succession to one another. As each society filled its list, a new one was started, and was able to assist the earlier ones, to the convenience of all. This led to the suggestion that a society might have a continuous existence with successive series of members, so that the membership should be terminable, but the society permanent. The plan was found to have other advantages. It was not necessary to fix one single term for the membership of every member. A man might subscribe for a 5 years' or 10 years' share as well as for a 14 years' share, or might pay up his share in full. A borrower might in like manner borrow for any term of years that suited his convenience. The terminating form of society held a member to his bargain until there was enough to pay out every other member the amount or value of his share. If losses occurred, this time might be prolonged. In any event, it could not be precisely ascertained beforehand. The permanent plan substituted for this a fixed contract for a definite term of years. Hence the amount payable by the society upon withdrawal of an unadvanced share, or by the member upon redemption of his mortgage, could be more accurately ascertained. The part of the question relating to possible losses was usually left in the background, but when it became necessary to find a solution for it, rules were made directing a deduction from the amount payable to members withdrawing in cases where these members had all the profits, and an additional payment by borrowers where they also shared in the profits. The permanent society therefore brought into high relief the differences between the investing class of member and the borrowing class, though the distinction in the Act was merely that of a share on which an advance has been made and a share on which an advance has not been made.

The business of a Building Society, legitimate and profitable as it was in general when it was restricted to the early intention of enabling each member to buy his own dwelling-house, took upon itself in many places by degrees a speculative character. Large sums were lent to builders and other persons who had not sufficient capital of their own to provide against the risks of the transaction. They fell into arrear with their repayments, and the society had ultimately to take the property into possession. Where it was situated in the suburbs of London or of some growing town, the centrifugal force which drives the inhabitants to seek their homes farther and farther from the centre came into operation, and the property declined in value. Where it was badly built, heavy charges for repair fell on the society. Many societies thus made losses and got into positions of difficulty.

Another cause of loss which too frequently came into

operation was direct peculation. In societies of this kind, much is necessarily left to the manager. If he happens to be a clever rogue, he will not have great difficulty in getting the control of the concern into his own hands. He is exposed to the temptation of frequently receiving large sums of money by way of redemption money, fully paid-up shares and the like, which a little astuteness, if there be no adequate supervision, may easily manipulate in the accounts or omit from them altogether. Yet the only provision in the Act of 1836 for audit was that it should be conducted by two of the members. Unless a society had a professional accountant among its members, it was compelled to elect as auditors persons who had not that qualification. To the lay auditor the necessity of many precautions, such as inspection of the mortgages and verification of the other securities, would rarely occur. No annual return was required to be sent to any public office. There was, accordingly, in many cases a complete lack of effective supervision, and the opportunity made the thief.

When, from these or other causes, winding up a society became urgent, it was found that nothing in the Acts of 1828 or 1834 met the case. The Companies Act 1862, contained provisions for winding up unregistered companies, sections 199 *et seq.*, and these entailed the most costly and burdensome form of procedure known to that Act. Every such winding up must be under the compulsory clauses, and must be proceeded with in the High Court of Chancery. When it was found that this was the only way of winding up an insolvent Building Society, it was evident that the disaster was made worse, and that little or nothing would be saved out of the wreck for the unfortunate members.

In 1870 these considerations had become so pressing that the managers of several large Building Societies formed themselves into a committee to draw up a bill to amend the law. That bill was submitted to the Royal Commission on Friendly Societies, and they proceeded to take evidence on the question, and made the amendment of the law of Building Societies the subject of their second Report, presented in 1872. Ultimately, the Building Societies Act 1874, was passed, carrying into effect some of the recommendations of the Royal Commission. These were, that the form of the Building Society (the prefix "benefit" might usefully be suppressed) as distinct from the joint-stock company, should be maintained; that the law on the subject should be consolidated and amended; that Building Societies should continue to be registered with the Registrar of Friendly Societies; that the certificate of registration should carry corporate powers; that the exemption from stamp-duty on mortgages should be limited (it was in the result wholly taken away); that the privilege of paying small sums on intestacy without letters of administration should be raised to a maximum of £50; that the privilege of priority against the estates of deceased debtors (that is, those who are officers holding funds by virtue of their office) should be abolished; that the rules should provide whether there shall be any power to borrow, and to what extent, within the limits fixed by the law, and whether preferential capital may be issued, and as to withdrawals and redemptions; that the limit of the borrowing power should be two-thirds of the total value of the amounts for the time being secured on mortgage, or, as an alternative for terminating societies, six (this became twelve) months' subscriptions; that societies should be required to produce their mortgages to the auditors; that the Registrar should be invested with power to settle disputes; that the enforcement of the law should be secured by an efficient system of penalties; and that other matters should be provided for, in particular, joint-membership.

The Act of 1874 left existing societies under the Acts of 1828, 1834, and 1836 until they should, on their own application, become incorporated under that of 1874. A casual error in an amendment made in the House of Lords caused it to express a different intention, but this was corrected by a short act passed in 1875. Later on, an amending act, of which we shall have to speak presently, repealed the Act of 1836, so far as regards societies established after 1856. The only societies, therefore, which now remain under the operation of the three old acts are those established before 1857 which have not become incorporated under the Act of 1874. Of these, 304 are not known to have ceased to exist, but only 71 are known to be in actual existence. None of these are in Scotland or Ireland.

The Act of 1874 also provided for making annual returns to the Registrar, and laid down the important requirements that the statement of the amount due upon mortgage securities as an asset is not to include prospective interest; it introduced a simple method of dissolving societies by means of an instrument of dissolution, signed by three-fourths of the members holding two-thirds of the shares; and restricted the right of applying to the Court (which was defined to be the County Court and not the Court of Chancery) for winding up compulsorily or under supervision to a judgment creditor for a sum exceeding £50, or a member authorized by a meeting of the society to present a petition.

Other amending acts were passed in 1877, 1884, and

1888 to remove doubts which had arisen as to matters of detail; but the policy of the law was not again brought under general review until the events occurred which led to the passing of the Act of 1894. During the intervening twenty years, in England and Wales, more than 600 old societies had been incorporated under the Act of 1874, and as many as 3351 new societies had been formed. Of these 1526 had ceased to exist. The Act had, it was evident, given rise to the formation of a great number of mushroom societies. The assets of Building Societies (old and new) under the Act of 1874 reached their highest point in 1890, when they were returned at £50,778,797. They dropped £196,432 in the return published in 1891; £869,363 in that published in 1892; £7,029,731 in that published in 1894. A similar though smaller diminution is shown in the return for Scotland and Ireland.

The explanation of this sudden cessation of apparent prosperity is found in the stoppage of the Liberator Building Society of London, one of the largest on the list, which had drawn its funds from provident persons in almost every class of society, who were led by specious representations to believe in its absolute safety. It appeared upon investigation that nearly all the legitimate Building Society business the society ever had had been converted into book entries against a number of other concerns under the same management, which shared in the general crash, and that every penny of the shareholders' capital had absolutely melted away. The aggregate losses in the whole of the concerns amounted to many millions of money, and in the Liberator alone exceeded one million. The misery and suffering caused by this failure were wide-spread and enormous; many who had relied upon their savings invested in these concerns found themselves destitute: some became paupers, some died in want or committed suicide in despair.

Other societies came to grief about the same time, and public confidence in Building Societies generally was severely shaken. A "run" was made upon several societies which had been in the habit of receiving deposits repayable on demand. In the case of the principal society of the class, the "Birkbeck", one of those established under the Act of 1836 before 1857, and not incorporated under the Act of 1874, it had its resources so largely invested in available securities that it was able to meet every claim; and the "run" strengthened the credit and reputation of the society instead of weakening it. With that exception, the loss of public confidence arising from the failure of the Liberator and other societies was so marked and so prejudicial to Building Societies generally that all parties were agreed that a considerable amendment of the Building Societies Acts was a matter of great urgency. In the session of 1893 as many as four bills were brought into the House of Commons for that purpose, and they were all referred to a select committee, of which Mr. Herbert Gladstone was chairman. Their deliberations resulted in the passing in the next session of the Building Societies Act 1894.

That Act conferred large and unusual powers upon the Registrar, to whom any three members may supply evidence by way of statutory declaration of facts which call for investigation, or for recourse to the judgment of a meeting of the members; and if the society fails to furnish a satisfactory explanation of such facts within fourteen days, the Registrar may appoint an inspector or may call a special meeting. He may also do so if one-tenth of the whole number of members in a small society, or 100 members in a society which consists of more than 1000 members, apply to him; and may do so of his own motion, if the society has been guilty of persistent neglect to make returns, or persistent neglect to correct or complete an inadequate return.

Any ten members, each of not less than twelve months' standing, may apply to the Registrar to appoint an accountant or actuary to inspect the books of a society and to report thereon. Upon proper application, also, the Registrar may dissolve a society, if it cannot meet the claims of the members, and if a dissolution would be for their benefit, and may direct the manner in which its affairs are to be wound up. This provision has been made available in a variety of circumstances. In the case of a society where the transactions were large, and an exhaustive investigation of the proceedings of the managers appeared to be called for, it was directed that the society should be wound up, as nearly as might be, in the same manner as if the Registrar's award of dissolution were an order of a court under the Companies Acts; in other cases, the direction has been for winding up in the same manner as if the award were an instrument of dissolution signed by the members; and in others, detailed directions have been given according to the circumstances of the case. He may cancel or suspend the registry of a society which persists in an illegal course after notice from the Registrar; and may take proceedings against societies to enforce the provisions of the Act, and against persons misapplying the funds of societies. For most of these purposes he has to obtain the approval of the Secretary of State.

Every society is required to include in its rules tables showing, in respect of unadvanced shares, the amount due by the society for principal and interest separately, and in respect of advanced shares the amount due from the borrower after each stipulated payment, unless the Registrar is of opinion that such tables are not applicable to the society. Except in the case, therefore, where the scheme of the society is such that no tables could be given—as, for example, the case of a society which makes its advances by sale—every member is able to find out by mere inspection of the table in his rules how much is due to him from the society at any given time, or how much it would cost him to redeem his mortgage. Under the old system it frequently happened that a society, after charging a member interest at a high rate for the whole term of his mortgage, would allow him discount at a low rate, so that if he desired to redeem, after having paid a considerable sum on account of principal, the society would still be able to claim from him as much as the original amount advanced, and sometimes even more. The society can do so still, but is not so likely to adopt that course when the result has to be printed in a table in the rules.

Every society is also required to make in its rules express provision as to how losses are to be ascertained and provided for, and when membership is to cease. Great injustice has been done to the members of societies where the rules have not contained provisions requiring members withdrawing to contribute to the losses incurred while they were members, as in the case of the decision of the House of Lords in *Auld* v. *The Glasgow Building Society*; and it is hoped that this may be avoided in future.

The society's power to borrow is considerably restricted by the provision that in calculating the limit of two-thirds of the amount secured to the society by mortgages from its members, mortgages more than twelve months in arrear, and mortgages on property of which the society has taken possession for twelve months, are not to be included. Schedules of such mortgages are to be appended to every annual statement of account, as well as of mortgages exceeding £5000; and the auditors are required to certify that the accounts are correct, duly vouched, and in accordance with law, and that they have in fact inspected all the mortgages, stating the number. The annual accounts and statements of societies are to be uniform.

While the measure was under consideration, it appeared desirable to obtain information as to the extent to which properties were held in possession by societies, and the House of Commons resolved, on the motion of the Right Hon. W. L. Jackson, to present an address to Her Majesty, asking for a return on the subject. Accordingly the Secretary of State addressed a request for the information to 2371 societies. In answer, 1436 societies stated that they had no properties in possession, and 716 stated that they had properties in possession which, in the aggregate, had been originally valued at £5,100,115, on which they had advanced £4,342,182, of which £4,120,457 was still due, and stood in their assets as £3,715,106. They derived a gross income during the year from rents, &c., amounting to £291,945, against which were to be reckoned outgoings amounting to £163,861. The remaining 219 societies withheld the information called for, although the Secretary of State more than once renewed his request for it.

It will be interesting to compare these figures with those for the year 1896, now that it has been made obligatory upon the societies to furnish the information.

The properties in possession now returned as assets amount to £5,526,804; and a comparison of the returns of individual societies with those for the year 1892 shows that during the four years the societies generally have unloaded themselves of a considerable portion of the properties in possession which they then held. An examination of the returns of the 219 societies which declined to furnish the information in 1892 leads to the conclusion that they had then in possession an amount at least equal to that returned by the other societies; in other words, that the properties in possession have been reduced in the four years from 7½ millions to 5½ millions.

This diminution of two millions is largely due to the indirect operation of the Act. It has no doubt been obtained at some cost, but in general it is the wiser course for a society boldly to face its losses. The remaining 5½ millions will probably not be realized without further loss, and will postpone for many societies the time when they can again become the profit-earning concerns that they used to be in the early years of the movement.

Besides the properties taken into possession, mortgages amounting to £509,036 had fallen into arrear for more than twelve months. The mortgages for sums exceeding £5000 amounted in the whole to £2,010,811. As the total mortgages held by 2360 incorporated societies in England and Wales are for £38,770,032, it follows that 14·3 per cent of the total are on properties in possession, 1·3 per cent are in arrear, 5·2 per cent are for large amounts, and 79·2 per cent are unaffected by these conditions and may be taken to represent the legitimate and profitable business of the societies.

Taking incorporated and unincorporated societies for

the whole of the United Kingdom, returns have been obtained from 2635 societies having 635,716 members. Their aggregate receipts during the financial year ending in 1897 were £33,306,638. Their assets were: balances due on mortgage, £43,350,439; other assets, £13,047,018; total, £56,397,457. Of this, shareholders' capital stood for £34,845,218; debts to depositors and others, £19,030,242; and net profit balances, £2,521,997.

If to these large figures, representing the existing business of building societies, we add the vast sums that during the last 60 years have been advanced to and repaid by their members, we shall have some idea of the marvellous extent of their beneficial operations. If we reduce the 43 millions due on mortgage by 20 per per cent, for large mortgages, mortgages in arrear, and properties in possession, we get a net sum of 35 millions. Taking the average mortgage at £300, the number of existing mortgages would be 115,000. Looking back on the whole history of Building Societies, it is certainly not too much to say that a quarter of a million persons have been able by their means to become the proprietors of their own homes.

To many a man among these the day when the repayments terminated and he was able henceforth to live in a house of his own, rent free, was a beginning of days of prosperity and comfort, leading in some cases to comparative opulence, or at least to such an amount of provident accumulation as to remove all cause of anxiety from the contemplation of approaching old age.

Chapter XII.

Savings-banks.

Savings-banks of the type now called Trustee Savings-banks, were well established before the Victorian era began, but that period has seen a wonderful development of them, and some change in their character. Daniel Defoe gave the first hint of them in his fruitful *Essay on Projects*, published in 1697. They took root on the continent of Europe before they began to be established in England. Between 1765 and 1796, Savings-banks were formed in Brunswick, Hamburg, Oldenburg, Berne, Loire, Basil, Geneva, and Kiel. In 1797 Bentham revived Defoe's suggestion under the name of "Frugality Banks", and in 1799 the first English Savings-bank was founded at Wendover in Bucks by the Rev. Joseph Smith. Miss Priscilla Wakefield had established a Friendly Society at Tottenham in Middlesex in 1798, and in 1801 she added a Savings-bank to it. Savings-banks were shortly after established in London, Bath, Dumfriesshire, Edinburgh, Kelso, Hawick, Southampton, and elsewhere. In the latter part of the eighteenth and beginning of the nineteenth century, methods of bettering the condition of the industrial population were much in men's minds, as we have already seen in connection with the history of Friendly Societies. Many well-intended measures were introduced into Parliament for making comprehensive provision for the poorer classes, especially with reference to their old age. These failing, the simple expedient of providing for the safe-keeping of small sums, and accumulating them at compound interest, was widely adopted. From the beginning to the present time, Savings-banks have been distinguished from all the other bodies which we have discussed in one important particular. They are managed for the depositors, not by the depositors. The management is exercised by a body of volunteers, in the election of whom the depositors have no voice. These persons, termed trustees and managers, are expressly prohibited by statute from deriving any remuneration or profit for themselves out of the transactions of the Savings-banks, and the name "Trustee Savings-banks" aptly marks out this distinguishing characteristic.

As the safety of the deposits is a matter of primary importance, it was from the first provided that they should be invested in government stock. In 1817, acts were passed to encourage the establishment of banks for savings in England and Ireland, and the government then undertook itself to receive the deposits from the trustees of the Savings-banks, through the Commissioners for the Reduction of the National Debt, into whose accounts at the Banks of England and Ireland the trustees were to pay in all they received. Upon these sums a fixed rate of interest of 3*d.* per day, or £4, 11s. 3*d.* per cent per annum, was to be paid; and the government undertook to return the deposits in full when required. This appears to be a high rate of interest; but it is to be remembered that for nearly forty years the price of government stock had then been so low that upon the average £4, 11*s.* 3*d.* could easily have been earned by investment in that security. Unfortunately for the Savings-bank fund, but fortunately for the nation at large, almost immediately after this, the tide turned. Our military and naval successes in the war with France re-established the credit of the country. Stock went up, and the Commissioners became unable to realize the rate of £4, 11*s.* 3*d.* per cent on their purchases. Each year, however, interest was credited upon the deposits, whether it had been earned or not. The result was, that a deficiency of capital accrued, taking the stock at its cost price. It shortly became evident that something must be done; and in 1828, the rate of interest was reduced to 2½*d.* per day, or £3, 16*s.* 0½*d.* per cent per annum. It is a pity that a sum had not been voted each year by Parliament to make up the deficiency in interest. The question never really affected the Savings-banks themselves, as the government accepted the responsibility of repaying the deposits at par, and therefore the depositors could lose nothing, but it was a bad principle in finance to leave the deficiency to accumulate instead of meeting each year's claim as it arose. The result of this financial error was that the income from the investments soon became insufficient to meet the claims for interest even at the reduced rate, inasmuch as it was derived from a diminished capital.

Meanwhile, the Savings-banks were largely increasing their business. The full government security for the amounts deposited with the Commissioners, and the liberal rate of interest allowed, made them exceedingly popular. By 1837, there were about 300 banks in existence, having about 600,000 depositors, and the amount to their credit was nearly 20 millions sterling, or about 15*s.* per head of the population of the country. The growth of the deficiency again forced itself on the attention of the legislature, and in 1850 the rate of interest was reduced to 2*d.* per diem, or £3, 0*s.* 10*d.* per annum. The defective financial system was not remedied till many years after, when the existing deficiency was provided for, and a vote is now taken annually for each year's deficiency as it arises. As in 1888 the rate of interest was again reduced to £2, 15*s.* per cent, there would now be little or no deficiency, if the government were not bound by its contracts with Friendly Societies. These were allowed to deposit their funds without limit with the National Debt Commissioners, and so long as any assurances exist, which were contracted for before 1828, 1850, and 1888 respectively, the Commissioners continue to pay the high rates of interest on the premiums received under these insurances.

The legislation as to Savings-banks in Scotland was somewhat later than that for England and Ireland. An act for their protection was passed in 1819, but it was not till 1835 that they were permitted to deposit their funds with the National Debt Commissioners. They came in consequence to be called "National Security" Savings-banks, but that name has now been discontinued; and the Consolidating Act of 1863 applies to Savings-banks in all parts of the United Kingdom.

Though the growth of the deficiency in the Savings-banks and Friendly Societies Fund arising from insufficiency of interest has now been stopped, there is another consideration which makes every contract by the government to accept deposits repayable on demand unfavourable to the State. The times when deposits are made and money has to be invested are times of general prosperity, when the funds are at a high price; the times when deposits are withdrawn, and money has to be withdrawn from investment, are times of general depression, when the funds are at a low price. Hence, the government has always to buy in the dearest market and sell in the cheapest. This is shown very clearly by the late Mr. Scratchley in an analysis of the transactions of the eighteen years from 1840 to 1858. During those quarters when the funds were at an average price of par, the deposits by trustees of Savings-banks with the Commissioners exceeded their withdrawals by £1,300,000; when the funds were at an average price of 96, deposits exceeded withdrawals by £2,000,000; when the funds fell to an average of 90¼, withdrawals exceeded deposits by more than 4½ millions, and when funds were as low as 83⅞, withdrawals exceeded deposits by more than 4 millions. This state of things affects the State only in its self-imposed office of banker to the trustees, and does not affect the trustees or the depositors.

A system thus grew up by which large sums of money were entrusted to the philanthropic and benevolent persons who took upon them the unpaid office of trustees and managers, upon condition that they should hand the money to the government, and that the depositors should get government security for it. The legislature sought in 1828 to restrict the benefits of the system to the poorer classes by limiting the amount that any one person might deposit to £30 in any one year, and £150 in the aggregate. There was a weak joint in the armour by which the depositors were to be protected from the risk of losing their money. Government was responsible for all that it received, but not for what it did not receive. Unpaid trustees and managers are apt to become negligent. Many disastrous cases arose in which the paid servant of the Savings-bank entered upon a career of fraud, continued it for years, and when he finally died or disappeared, or some accident caused his detection, it was found, to the dismay of the trustees and managers, as well as of the unfortunate depositors, that the funds that had been paid over to the National Debt Commissioners were less by many thousands of pounds than the amount which had been received from the depositors. For these deficiencies the government was in no way responsible. Thus, in 1848 a Savings-bank in Cuffe Street, Dublin, closed with a deficiency of £56,000; in the same year, one in Tralee, with £36,000, and about the same time, another in Killarney. In 1849, the actuary of the Savings-bank at Rochdale died, in high repute for honesty, probity, and wealth. It was then found that out of £100,403 received by the bank, only £28,626 was left, the actuary having misappropriated £71,717. Other smaller cases came to light at various times, the latest important one being that at Cardiff, which was investigated by the Hon. Lyulph Stanley, and ultimately wound up in the Chancery Division of the High Court under an act passed in 1891 enabling insolvent Savings-banks thus to be dealt with.

The loss to the depositors was in some cases mitigated by personal responsibility having been established against the trustees or voluntarily assumed by them; but this did not avail in all cases to meet the whole of the deficiency, and where it was not so, and heavy loss fell upon the depositors, the Trustee Savings-banks failed in their primary object of the "safe custody" of the deposits, and this caused wide-spread distrust of their system and a feeling of insecurity among depositors generally. The liability of these gratuitous trustees beyond that for their own acts is limited to cases where they fail to take security from their officers, or to maintain the checks which are required by the Act of 1863. Altogether, it seems probable that losses to the amount of near £200,000 have had to be borne by depositors in Savings-banks. Though this is a small amount as compared with the enormous sums that have been deposited, its moral effect is great. Two measures have been taken in consequence. The first is the establishment by Mr. Gladstone in 1861 of the system of Post-office Savings-banks, to which we shall refer in the next chapter, by which every deposit, as soon as it is made to the local postmaster, is fully guaranteed by government. The second is the establishment in 1891 of the Inspection Committee of Trustee Savings-banks, by which the requirements of the Statute are enforced upon negligent trustees. This latter measure has been so successful, that whereas in 1892, the inspectors employed reported that in 167 Savings-banks, 608 instances of neglect of statutory requirements had been discovered, the inspectors in 1896 visited the whole of the 245 Savings-banks then existing, and found in all of them only 219 such instances.

The effect of the establishment of the Post-office Savings-bank has been to stop the formation of new Trustee Savings-banks, and to cause the dissolution of many old ones. In 1861, when the Post-office Bank was commenced, there were 640 Trustee Banks; there are now only 239. The business of the Trustee Savings-banks has not, however, diminished to any great extent; the 20 millions of 1837 having increased to 45 millions, though such increase is largely due to the accumulation of interest. It may be said generally that the Post-office Savings-bank has not so much drawn business away from the old banks as it has opened out new facilities for saving, and obtained fresh business for itself.

The Inspection Committee, which was created in 1891, is not a government department. A majority of its members are representatives of the Savings-banks themselves, and the others are an officer of the Bank of England, representatives of the Institute of Chartered

Accountants and the Law Institution, and a member appointed by the Chief Registrar of Friendly Societies. The chairman is Sir Albert Rollit, M.P., who represents the important Savings-bank at Hull. The principle of its constitution is to throw upon the Savings-banks the responsibility of themselves devising means to safeguard the deposits, and to provide them with the assistance of a small body of experts to enable them to discharge it.

Besides the formal inspection of the banks by accountants appointed by the committee, which at first extended over two or three years, and is now completely made every year, the committee has prepared a set of model rules which it recommends Savings-banks to adopt by way of complete amendment of their existing rules; has framed regulations by which the auditors are required to inspect a certain number of the pass-books of depositors on each occasion of audit; has taken measures to enforce the requirements of the law upon negligent trustees; and has especially watched over the proceedings of those Savings-banks which have what are called special investment departments.

These special investments arise from a provision of Section 12 of the Act of 1827 that it should not prevent the trustees of a Savings-bank receiving from any depositor sums for a specific purpose of investment. The object of this provision appears to have been that when a depositor had accumulated as much in his ordinary Savings-bank account as was allowed (which at that time was £150 only) the trustees should be permitted to invest any further sums for him in stock, so as to save him the trouble of instructing a broker, and the risk of being tempted to spend his money. It was so understood for many years, though only one important bank, that at Exeter, allowed the depositors to avail themselves of the privilege. The section was re-enacted in the Act of 1863 as section 16, and that seems to have drawn the attention of managers of Savings-banks to the facilities it affords for helping those depositors who have more than they are allowed to invest in the ordinary way, or desire higher interest than the bank can pay on its ordinary deposits. In respect of such investments the trustees are equally bound to act gratuitously as in relation to the ordinary business of the bank; but the investment is entirely at the depositors' risk, and wholly for his benefit. Several Savings-banks adopted rules enabling them to open special investment departments, in which, instead of taking the depositors' express instructions as to the investment, and earmarking the stock bought by his deposit on his behalf, they received sums from any number of depositors, paying withdrawals out of receipts, and investing the balance on such securities as the trustees thought fit. The interest earned was distributed each year among the several depositors, but frequently a reserve was kept to meet contingencies and provide for equalizing dividends, so that in fact the business became that of an ordinary deposit bank granting interest on deposits at an agreed rate.

By the Acts of 1827 and 1863 these transactions were left wholly unregulated, but in 1891, when the act establishing the Inspection Committee was passed, the legislature thought fit to prohibit the opening any special investment branch by any Savings-bank which had not one already, and to stringently regulate the special investments of those which were allowed to continue the business. This led to several banks closing their special investment branches. Those that remain are now only 14 in number, having 40,410 accounts, and £4,952,260 invested. The closing of the special investment business has led to some curious questions. The plan of keeping a reserve for future contingencies raised a difficulty, inasmuch as the trustees are bound to hold all the produce of the investment for the benefit of the several depositors. As these reserve funds are undoubtedly part of the interest earned by the investments, they clearly belong to the depositors, and the question arose, how were they to be distributed among them. Many depositors had closed their accounts. Some, it was alleged, had given a full discharge to the trustees. Where a profit arose on realizing the securities, other questions had to be settled. It clearly belonged to the depositors, by whose money the securities had been bought; but no particular security could possibly be earmarked as derived from any particular deposit, inasmuch as a running account of receipts and withdrawals was kept, and only the surplus invested. Fortunately, the legislature had provided a cheap and easy method of settling all disputes by reference to the Registrar of Friendly Societies, and had enacted that there should be no appeal from the decision. On such a case being brought before the Registrar, it was held that the gain arising from excess of interest belonged to all the depositors, and should be distributed among them in proportion to the amount distributed by way of interest; and that the gain arising from profit on realization belonged only to such depositors as remained until the close, those who withdrew earlier being taken to have elected to accept their money at par. Upon these lines, it was possible to draw up a simple scheme of application of the surplus fund which equitably distributed it among the past and present depositors according to their respective interests.

A few specimens of the disputes which are settled by the Registrar under the provisions of the Trustee Savings-banks Acts may be interesting. £50 was deposited in 1838, by someone whose name is not known, for the repair of a school in the parish of C. The school then in operation ceased to exist in 1852, and the trustees of the fund are long since deceased. Another school for the parish was founded in 1850. That school is now existing, and the Registrar felt justified in awarding that the deposits be applied to the repairs of the existing school. A charity was founded about sixty years ago, without trust deed or written constitution of any sort. The trustees desired that the funds should be dealt with by the rector and churchwardens of the parish, and the Registrar made an award that the deposits be paid to them accordingly. A depositor died in 1892, leaving a child dependent upon her relatives. Her husband had left her in 1883, and had contributed nothing to the support of the child. The Registrar awarded that the deposits should be applied for the maintenance and benefit of the child. The vicar of a parish in 1874 induced the members of an old Benefit Club to register it and deposit its money in the Savings-bank, but the members did not take kindly to the new system and gradually dropped off. The rector died, and the surviving trustees refused to act. The Registrar caused inquiry to be made as to the persons who had been members, and made an award distributing the funds among them. Many cases of interest arise out of claims of the guardians of the poor to money deposited by, or on behalf of, persons who became chargeable to them; others out of claims by creditors who have obtained judgment against debtors and cannot get satisfaction without recourse to the deposit account; others where depositors or persons entitled to deposits have not been heard of for more than seven years and are presumed to be dead. In some cases, disputes arise where, for some reason or other, a person has made deposits in the name of some other person, and afterwards desires to recover the money, or where a person entrusts another with money to deposit on his behalf. The vicar of a parish collected money for a missionary society and deposited it in the Savings-bank in his name as treasurer of the society. He in due course paid the money collected to the society out of his own funds, but did not withdraw it from the Savings-bank, where it remained at his death, when the question arose, Did the money belong to the society or to his estate. It was found that it belonged to the estate, and was ordered to be paid to the executors. The treasurer of a small Provident Society of workmen paid in its funds to the Savings-bank. Upon his death, his successor in office applied, on behalf of all the subscribers, that the money should be paid to his widow, in sympathy with her at the loss of her husband.

The rules of some Savings-banks contain a provision that in case no claim is made within a certain time after the death of a depositor, the deposits are to be transferred to the surplus fund. The Registrar has held that such a rule is not valid, being contrary to several sections of the Act, and that its having been certified does not make it binding upon the depositors, even if they have given their written consent to be bound by the rules. This becomes an important matter when a Savings-bank is wound up, and the depositors who have not claimed their money are transferred to the Post-office. It is now necessary that the Savings-bank should pay over to the Post-office the amount of the deposits, which, if such a rule had been valid, would have been transferred to the surplus fund. There is, in fact, no statute of limitation applicable to Savings-bank deposits, and a Savings-bank is not at liberty to make one for itself. The trustees are only discharged from their responsibility for a deposit once made by the receipt of the depositor or of the person lawfully claiming through him, or by the award of the Registrar directing payment to any person. Cases frequently arise of deposits being claimed after many years.

The authority of the Registrar to settle disputes extends to deposits in the Post-office Savings-bank, and we shall therefore have another opportunity of referring to the interesting cases that frequently arise.

The 239 Trustee Savings-banks had 1,495,903 depositors on 20th Nov. 1896, and their deposits amounted to £46,699,687. The assets of the banks were £47,665,024. If to these be added the investments in stock on behalf of individual depositors, £1,082,248, and the special investments already referred to, the total amount of the assets of Trustee Savings-banks is £53,699,532. It may be mentioned that the Trustee Savings-banks in Glasgow, Liverpool, and Manchester have an organization of Penny Banks attached to them in the various elementary schools of the town, in which the children and others are encouraged to deposit small savings, with the provision that when the deposit reaches a certain amount, it shall be exchanged for a deposit-book of the Savings-bank. The Penny Banks of Liverpool, which have been organized very successby Mr. T. Banner Newton, the able actuary of the Liverpool Savings-bank, have effected a million transactions in a single year. This may serve to show the tendency of any sound movement to throw out vigorous offshoots. Though, in a certain sense, the Savings-bank is a rudimentary instrument of thrift as compared with the self-governing bodies, which are not only media for profitable investment of small capitals, but also valuable as an education in the knowledge of affairs, yet it has been of infinite use to many whose savings without it would not have been made, or would have been lost or squandered.

Chapter XIII.

Post-office Savings-banks.

We have seen that about the year 1860 the system of the Trustee Savings-banks had fallen somewhat under a cloud. The frauds were an undoubted blot upon it; and the deficiency in the stock held by the National Debt Commissioners, though the Savings-banks were in no way to blame, prejudiced the public mind. People began to think whether a plan by which the direct security of the government could be given to every depositor from the moment he made his deposit, and the rate of interest might be fixed so low as to be not beyond that earned, could not be devised. The idea of using the Post-office for these purposes was not a new one; it had been thrown out as early as 1807 by Mr. Whitbread; but the credit of reviving it, and making the public familiar with it, was due to Sir Charles Sikes of the Huddersfield Joint-stock Bank. The credit of adopting it was due to Mr. Gladstone, who made a memorable speech on the second reading of the bill, and to the Postmaster-General of his government, Lord

Stanley of Alderley. They had the valuable assistance of Mr. George Chetwynd and Mr. Frank Ives Scudamore in elaborating the details. The preliminary report of Mr. Chetwynd, on 30th Nov. 1860, the observations thereon, and financial estimates of Mr. Scudamore, dated 7th Jan. 1861, and the subsequent reports of both gentlemen, when the Post-office Savings-banks Act had been passed, on the arrangements to be made for putting it into operation, dated 30th July and 13th September, 1861, are masterly documents. The system they then laid down has been continued in its main features to the present day.

The Act was passed on the 17th May, 1861, and recites that "it is expedient to enlarge the facilities now available for the deposit of small savings, and to make the General Post-office available for that purpose, and to give the direct security of the State to every such depositor for repayment of all moneys so deposited by him, together with the interest due thereon". It was not contemplated that the new banks would at once supersede the old ones, and the result has shown that they have not done so, but have opened up new sources of saving, and directed them into a different channel. The position of the Post-office Bank differs in several respects from that of a Trustee Savings-bank. A depositor in a Trustee Savings-bank pays his money to the officer appointed to receive it, who enters it in the deposit-book, which is handed to the manager or check officer (as the Act requires two persons to be present at every transaction with a depositor, so as to form a double check), who transcribes the entry into a check-book kept by himself, which is verified with the cash at the closing of the bank for the day. The book is handed back to the depositor, and the transaction is complete. A like procedure is adopted in case of withdrawal, except that where the amount to be withdrawn is large, a previous notice has to be given. In the Post-office Savings-bank the depositor pays the money to the local postmaster, who enters it in the deposit-book, and also on a record of the day's transactions, and returns the deposit-book to the depositor. The record is sent at the close of the day to the head office of the Savings-bank Department in London, and there entries are made in the ledgers, and an acknowledgment sent to every depositor by post. Thus the entry by the local postmaster in the deposit-book is only a temporary acknowledgment: the final acknowledgment is that on a separate slip of paper, which is sent through the post to the depositor. In cases of withdrawal, the depositor obtains a form of notice from the local postmaster, and transmits it filled up and signed to the Savings-bank Department. A warrant is then made out in that department, after comparison of the signature to the notice with the signature of the depositor to the declaration made on opening the account, and sent to the depositor by post. This warrant is made payable at the local post-office specified by the depositor in the notice, where the depositor attends, and, having signed the warrant, receives the money. The local postmaster enters the payment in his record, which is transmitted at the end of the day to the Savings-bank Department, and there entered in the ledgers. These form a vast number of volumes, kept by a large staff of male and female clerks. Where there appears any reason for doing so, the local postmaster is instructed, when a warrant is issued, by a separate communication from the Department, to see that it is paid to the right person. The precautions thus taken are necessary to secure the safety of the deposits, and to prevent frauds upon depositors or upon the public by local postmasters and their assistants or other persons.

Some curious cases of dispute have arisen where the entry in the deposit-book and the acknowledgment from the chief office have not agreed. A young lady made a deposit which was entered in her book as £6, but only £5 was entered on the record sent to the department. She maintained that it was £6, and an award was made in her favour. A young man placed a coin on the counter of the local post-office, which was entered in his deposit-book as £1, but as soon as he had left the room was found to be a half-sovereign only; 10*s.* was entered on the record, and the fact reported. The depositor asserted that he had actually paid £1, but his statement was not accepted. The mother of a depositor sent certain money in June, 1892, to be paid to her credit, which was entered in the deposit-book as £16, but on the record as £6, 10*s.* only, and the acknowledgment from the chief office was accordingly for £6, 10*s.*, and not for £16; this acknowledgment was put aside unopened. On the deposit-book being sent to the chief office for examination in the following February, the discrepancy was discovered. The mother, who was the wife of a tradesman in a large way of business, stated that it was her practice to save all the crown pieces she received for the benefit of her children, and that the sum in question consisted of a number of such crown pieces, a £5 note, and a sovereign: that she examined the deposit-book as soon as her messenger brought it back, and told him that it was correct. After much evidence had been taken, it was held that the entry in the deposit-book must be taken to be correct, and an award was made accordingly.

It follows from these cases that depositors should be very careful—

1. To examine their deposit-books before leaving the post-office, and see that the entries are correct.
2. To examine the acknowledgments they receive from the Savings-bank Department.
3. To preserve those acknowledgments, as they, and not the deposit-book, are conclusive evidence against the Postmaster-General.

Other interesting cases have arisen in respect of withdrawals. A depositor gave notice of withdrawal for £16, received and signed a warrant for £16; the payment of £16 was entered in her deposit-book; yet she said she had only received £10, that she meant the figure £16 in the notice of withdrawal to stand for £10; that when she signed the warrant, the office was rather dark, and although asked to sign again after the gas had been lit, did not on either occasion observe the figure £16, though her second signature was immediately under it, and did not become aware until some weeks afterwards that £16 was entered in the book. The officers at the local post-office recollected having paid 16 sovereigns, and it was awarded that the depositor had not shown that she had not received that amount.

A depositor made, on 3rd July, 1890, a withdrawal, which was entered in her book as £50, and signed a receipt, on which fifty pounds was clearly written in words and figures. She nevertheless, in 1895, stated positively that she had only asked for £5 and only received £5; that when she signed the receipt she did not observe the amount written upon it; that she did not observe that £50 was entered against her in her deposit-book at the time, nor on 24th October, when she paid in £7; nor on 17th January, 1891, when she paid in £5, 10*s*., nor on 11th August, when she withdrew £35; nor on numerous occasions when she sent her book to be examined and credited with interest. She had married on 13th July, 1890, and separated from her husband twelve months afterwards; but both agreed that no sum exceeding £5 was necessary to be drawn for any expenses incurred by her on her marriage. She first found out the alleged error about two years after, and did not complain to the Controller of the Savings-bank Department until three years after that. It was held that the receipt for £50 was a good discharge to the Postmaster-General; that after so long a delay, the entry in the deposit-book could not be impeached except by cogent evidence; and that the evidence of the depositor, by itself, was not sufficient. An award was made against her accordingly; and it was shortly afterwards found that she had really received £50, and had immediately thereupon deposited £45 of it with a bank, where it had remained untouched, and had been utterly forgotten by her.

An inmate of the social wing of the Salvation Army left their depôt to enter a lunatic asylum, leaving his book in a locker, the key of which he kept. On his discharge, he found that the locker had been broken open, the book stolen, and the money withdrawn by a notice and warrant signed with his name. As these were forgeries, they were no discharge to the Postmaster-general, and an award was made for payment.

A female depositor was married in October, 1891. In February, 1892, she made a withdrawal. In May she made another, and then found that a leaf had been replaced in her book which was not there when the February withdrawal had been made, and which contained an entry that had been erased with a knife. Inquiries being made, it was discovered that the erased entry related to a withdrawal of £30 in November, 1891. The notice of withdrawal and warrant were signed in the married name of the depositor, and the person receiving the money was also required to sign a fresh declaration, in consequence of the change from the depositor's maiden name to her married name. These three signatures were all forgeries. An award was made for payment of the £30 with interest to the depositor.

In September and October, 1894, the local postmaster induced the fifteen-year-old daughter of a depositor to sign her mother's name to notices of withdrawal, and appropriated the money to his own use. Upon the forgery being detected, he induced the girl to throw the blame upon her father. An award was made for payment of the money to the depositor.

Many other cases of interest have arisen, of which we can only give a few examples. A valuable privilege which Savings-bank depositors enjoy in common with members of Friendly Societies, Co-operative Societies, and Trade-unions, is that of nominating the person who is to receive the deposits on the death of the depositor. A nomination cannot be made of any sum exceeding £100. It is evident that the directions of the regulations as to nominations must be closely followed. Thus, where a depositor wrote on a blank leaf of his deposit-book: "I wish my brother William to have the money what is due to me at my death"—that did not operate as a nomination, and the money had to be paid to the administrators of the estate of the deceased. On the other hand, a mere allegation by the executor that the nominee had been incorrectly described, when there was no question as to his identity, did not invalidate the nomination. Where a depositor had made a valid nomination under the Act of 1883, and being desirous that it should take effect as if made under the regulations of 1888, revoked it, and made another nomination in precisely the same terms, and it was alleged that this revocation and renomination were void, not having been signed in the presence of the persons whose names were subscribed as witnesses, it was held that the revocation and renomination were only so in form, and that in substance what happened was a confirmation of the original nomination, which had never become invalid. The defect in the attestation, even if provable in evidence, which is doubtful, did not affect the validity of such a confirmation, which required no attestation.

A telegraph messenger, though a married man, made a nomination in favour of his father, and on the death of the father, revoked it and made another in favour of his mother. When he was near death, he expressed some trouble about provision for his wife, and called for writing materials, but the nomination was never revoked. After urging the parties to come to terms, the Registrar was compelled to make an award in favour of the nominee. Where a nominee is an infant, the money is payable to him at the age of 16, but not earlier. In a case where a nominee was only 11 years of age at the death of the nominator, a claim was put in against the deposits when he reached the age of 16 for past maintenance, and an application was made by a relative that in the nominee's own interest the payment might be postponed till he was older. The claim for maintenance was rejected, but the nominee consented that an award by which he should receive the amount due to him by instalments would be to his own advantage, and an award was made accordingly. In a case where a depositor made a nomination in 1890 and a will in 1893, and where the estate not affected by the nomination was insufficient to pay the debts and testamentary expenses, the Registrar held that the will could not override the nomination; but that the nomination could not avail to defeat the lawful claims of creditors, including the claim of the executors for funeral and testamentary expenses. It was awarded accordingly that after payment of these claims, the balance of the deposits should be payable to the nominee.

In order that deposits in Savings-banks should be as much as possible restricted to persons belonging to the industrious classes, it was provided that no depositor (other than a Friendly or Provident Society) should deposit more than £30, afterwards increased to £50, in one year, or more than £150, afterwards increased to £200, in the whole; and in order to ensure compliance with this enactment, that a declaration should be made by each depositor on opening an account that he had no account in any other Savings-bank, and that if such declaration were false, or if a depositor infringed these limits, he should incur the penalty of forfeiture of the whole of the deposits. This was afterwards modified by a provision that the forfeiture should only be incurred if the barrister should be of opinion that the offence had been committed with a fraudulent intention. In 1891 it was still further modified by a provision that the forfeiture should only apply to such portions of the deposits illegally made, as the Postmaster-General or the National Debt Commissioners should think just in all the circumstances of the case. The original penalty of forfeiture of the whole deposits was out of all proportion to the magnitude of the offence. So obvious was this that on one occasion (in Ireland), where a forfeiture of £2000 had been incurred, Parliament voted £1000 towards mitigating the penalty. It is now in practice restricted within reasonable limits. The prohibition of double deposits has given rise to some curious cases. A man died apparently in great poverty in a room in Whitechapel. His effects, apart from money and securities for money, were valued at 5*s.*, but in his room were found £20 in cash, and a number of deposit receipts, notes, and Building Societies' pass-books to the value of £2600 and upwards. He had an account in the Blomfield Street Savings-bank in his own name, and another in the Post-office (transferred from the Whitechapel) Savings-bank with a fictitious Christian name. The latter amounted to £170, 12*s.* 11*d.* On the death of a man whose name was James M'P——, deposit-books of the Post-office Savings-bank in the name of John M'P—— for £146, 12*s.* 10*d.*, and of the Liverpool Savings-bank in the name of Patrick M'P—— for £30 were found among his papers, both opened by himself in the names of brothers who had been dead for more than twenty years.

A depositor who already had an account of her own, opened another as a joint account between herself (omitting her first Christian name) and her daughter-in-law (by her maiden name). A depositor on the morning of 7th August, 1894, paid in £20 to an account which he had opened that year, and to which £30 had been already paid in. On the afternoon of the same day he sent his daughter with his book to the same post-office to deposit £50. She was told that no more could be paid in to her father's account, and opened an account in her own name, though advised that her father might invest it in Government stock. Differences arose between them, when the father claimed the money as his, and the daughter asserted that it had been given to her as remuneration for services. The father admitted that she had rendered services without remuneration, and a reasonable sum was awarded to the daughter, the remainder being declared to be the money of the father, subject to any forfeiture he had incurred.

A Savings-bank deposit is not transferable, except in the manner provided by the regulations. It is not available as a security for a loan or other debt. The possession of the deposit-book gives no title to the deposits. The statutes and regulations prescribe to whom a deposit shall be payable. Cases arise, however, in which it becomes necessary to inquire who is the real owner of a deposit, and the Registrar has to make an award accordingly. The son of a mother, who had unhappily contracted drunken habits, induced her to sign a notice of withdrawal of her deposits and an authority for payment to himself, and then deposited a portion of the money in his own name. He promised to maintain her, but did not fulfil the promise. It was shown that the money, though deposited in the mother's name, really belonged to the father, and successive awards were made applying the money in the manner most beneficial to the father and mother. A young man having in his possession money belonging to a young woman to whom he was engaged to be married, and who was on her death-bed, deposited it in his own name, and claimed it as his. His claim was shown to be without foundation, and the deposits were ordered to be paid to the brother and sister of the deceased. A mother retained the deposit-book of a daughter who had left home, and made deposits of her own money in the account. This was admitted by the daughter, and the deposits ordered to be paid to the mother. A father who received a gratuity on retirement from the public service, placed it in the care of one daughter, who gave some of the money to another, who deposited it in her own name in trust for a third daughter, without the knowledge or consent of the father, in favour of whom an award was made. A son gave his father money to deposit for him, and he deposited it in his own name; an award was made for payment to the son. The purchaser of a Post-office policy paid the premium into the account of the person whose life was insured, who refused to consent to the transfer of the money unless paid for doing so, so that the purchaser had to pay it over again to prevent the policy lapsing; and an award was made in his favour for the return of the money. A woman with whom £106 had been placed by her mother-in-law for safe custody, deposited some of it in her own name and induced another woman to deposit some of it in hers; and an award was made for payment of the balances to the mother-in-law.

Many other cases might be cited from the records of the references to the Registrar, which have been several thousands in number, but these may suffice as specimens of the strange circumstances in which Savings-bank deposits are frequently made, and the curious questions to which they give rise. The Post-office Savings-bank was, from the first, a conspicuous success, and its business has continuously increased to the present time. Local post-offices, at which deposits may be made, are to be found in every town and almost every village in the kingdom; they are open daily for the receipt of deposits during all the hours in which the postal business is carried on; and thus facilities for making deposits are brought within the reach of every one. The complete guarantee of the Government for the safety of the deposits is given from the moment they are made; so that if, as in some of the cases we have mentioned, the local postmaster is fraudulent or careless, the depositor's claim on the Postmaster-general is fully acknowledged. So excellent is the organization, however, that the cases of fraud, not affecting the depositor, but the public who have to make up for the defalcation, have been few and trifling. Their total amount would be represented by an insignificant fraction of the annual rate of interest.

One of the fundamental principles which were laid down when the Post-office Savings-bank was established,—viz. that it should be self-supporting—is about to receive a severe strain, and the authorities will probably soon be called upon to consider whether any and what measures should be adopted. The rate of interest is now fixed at £2, 10*s*. per cent, and the expenses of management add a fractional amount to that rate. Consols have been reduced to 2¾ per cent, and are about to be reduced to 2½, and yet the national credit is so good that the market price of consols is much above par. It will shortly become impossible for the interest paid to be earned by an investment in government stock, and the question will then have to be determined whether the rate of interest generally shall be reduced, or whether other investments of less security should be made. We believe the first alternative, if adopted, will in no appreciable degree affect the popularity of the Post-office Savings-bank, which depends much more largely on the security it offers than on the promise of high interest. If that is not so, if there is to any extent a practice of depositing money with the Post-office for the purpose of getting higher interest for it than can be got in the market, which we do not think credible, that would be only another reason why the reform should be effected, for such deposits are not desirable from any point of view.

The Post-office, like some of the large Trustee Savings-banks to which we have referred, assists in the organization of Penny Savings-banks, and supplies them with forms and directions. By the system of stamp cards for deposits, and in many other ways, it has sought to promote thrift. It is an agent for the purchase and sale of stock for depositors, and in conjunction with the Commissioners for the Reduction of the National Debt it does a large business—though perhaps not so large as is to be desired—in connection with Government Life Assurances and Government Immediate and Deferred Annuities.

A History of the Post-office Savings-bank, appended to the 43rd Report of the Postmaster-general, speaks of the impetus given to its work by the late Mr. Fawcett, who became Postmaster-general in 1880. "It was his constant endeavour, by speech and pamphlet, to make the system familiar and acceptable to all classes of the people. Under his direction the annuity and insurance business of the Post-office became a part of the Savings-bank system, and the Savings-bank also began to act as agent for persons of small means who might desire to deposit in the national funds. The ordinary business of the Savings-bank owes to him the rapid increase of branch offices in the villages; the special attention paid to bodies of navvies and workmen at their places of employment; and above all, the arrangement for making small deposits by slips of postage stamps." The number of such stamp slip deposits was, in 1896, 1,741,000, and their amount £95,000.

In 1891, the maximum amount of deposits was raised from £150 to £200, and in 1893 the annual limit was raised from £30 to £50. In 1893 also arrangements were made for withdrawal of money by telegraph. In 1896, 102,500 such withdrawals were made. It is understood that the precautions against the risk of fraud on these transactions have been successful.

At the close of the year 1896 there were 11,867 Post-office Savings-banks open. The number of deposit accounts was 6,862,035, and the amount standing to their credit was £108,098,641; the average amount standing to the credit of each account being £15, 15*s*. The number of transactions during the year was seventeen millions, being 12,638,307 deposits amounting to £36,258,350, and 4,367,594 withdrawals amounting to £28,489,329. £2,460,645 was credited to the depositors for interest. The expenses of management amounted to 6*d*. upon each transaction, or 7*s*. 11¼*d*. per cent of the total amount of deposits. In both respects there has been a steady diminution. The Postmaster-general is justified in saying that "these figures speak eloquently of the popularity of the Post-office Savings-bank and of the place which it has taken in the social economy of the nation".

Chapter XIV.

Other Provident Societies.

Among the measures which have been taken by the employers of labour for the benefit of their workmen, Railway Savings-banks deserve to be prominently mentioned. The Manchester, Sheffield, and Lincolnshire Railway Company established such a bank in 1860, and it has now 4341 depositors with a capital of £546,089, or £126 to each depositor. The South-Eastern Railway Savings-bank, established 1869, has an even larger number of depositors, numbering 4530, for a capital of £386,893 or £85 to each. The Caledonian, established 1874, exceeds these figures, for it has 4699 depositors of £515,000, or £109 for each. The Great Eastern, dating from 1878, heads the list in regard to number of depositors, having 4981 with £235,322 capital, or £47 to each.

The 16 Railway Savings-banks, of which 5 are in Scotland and the remainder in England, have, in the aggregate 37,087 depositors, and a capital of £3,124,069, an increase in a single year of 3948 depositors and more than £270,000 capital. The transactions of the year appear to have been 185,000 deposits amounting to £640,000, and 25,000 withdrawals amounting to £475,000. Interest was added at an average rate of $3^5/_6$ per cent.

The persons who are admitted to deposit in these banks are the employees of the company and their near relatives. Accounts are sometimes opened for benefit clubs and other societies established among the workmen; but the funds of a registered Friendly Society cannot lawfully be deposited in a Railway Savings-bank. There is no restriction to the amount of each depositor's holding; and the figures given above show that the privilege of depositing large sums is freely used. The average amount of each deposit account in the 16 banks exceeds £84—a sum which contrasts with the Post-office average of £15, 15*s*.

The funds are deposited with the railway company, and are, in general, secured upon the profits of the undertaking, next after the charges for debenture stock. The high rate of interest is no doubt an attraction to depositors. It is at the same time a substantial benefit to the employees of the company, and the figures show that they appreciate it. That 37,000 workmen in a single branch of industry have entrusted their employers with savings amounting to more than three millions sterling is a remarkable fact.

As the establishment of Savings-banks is virtually an extension of the borrowing powers of the companies, it is obvious that it should not be authorized by statute except under proper conditions. For this purpose a clause was drawn up by Mr. Ludlow in 1876, and has been inserted (subject to such slight modifications as have been required by changes in the acts of parliament referred to therein) in every private act since promoted by a railway company for the establishment of Railway Savings-banks.

This clause confers upon the banks and depositors certain privileges, such as that of nomination for sums payable at death, and of the settlement of disputes by the Registrar of Friendly Societies. It requires the companies to make and register proper rules, and to furnish annual accounts to the depositors and the public. The Railway Savings-bank is, in the case of several companies, only one of a number of large and liberal organizations mainly supported by them in the interests of their workmen. Of many companies it may be said that the directors show a praiseworthy desire to be models to other employers of labour in respect of the enlightened interest they take in methods of promoting the welfare of those they employ. The sums of money accumulated at a high rate of interest, which amount in two companies to averages of £109 and £126, and in cases of individual deposits must exceed even those amounts, must form to the depositors a substantial provision for the future.

It is not improbable that similar arrangements exist between employer and workman in other branches of industry, but escape public notice, as the industries concerned are not, like railways, regulated by act of parliament. A notable example is afforded by the arrangements made by Mr. Livesey, the manager of the South Metropolitan Gas Company, for the benefit of its workmen.

The legislature has also been moved of late years to grant parliamentary powers to numerous municipal corporations for the establishment of thrift funds for the benefit of the persons employed by them. Some such funds have indeed existed for a considerable period of years; but in those cases they were entered upon without much consideration of the probable ultimate burden that would fall upon the ratepayers, and were merely arrangements by which, in consideration of a small deduction from wages or salaries, retiring pensions would be promised to the officers and servants. More recently, it has become common to insert in the general powers bills of corporations provisions of this kind; and the committees of both houses of parliament, by whom these bills have been considered, have given careful attention to the nature of the safeguards that should be introduced into them. These have been settled in the case of the Cardiff Corporation Act 1894, and other subsequent acts, and will probably be adopted in the event of bills of the same kind being presented by other corporations in the future. The general scheme of these measures is that the employees submit to a deduction from their salaries or wages, usually not exceeding 2½ per cent, and that the corporation guarantee pensions to them at a rate to be fixed in a scheme to be framed after consultation with an actuary. It is also in general provided that at stated intervals there shall be actuarial valuations made of the funds and of the liabilities of the corporation. This is a very essential provision, as otherwise the rate-payers would have no knowledge of the extent of the responsibility they were accepting to be liquidated in future years. The only principle upon which a municipal corporation or other public body, or indeed any private employer, should undertake to pay pensions to the persons employed, is the principle of deferred pay.

The payments made to any person employed, whether by salary or by pension, cannot be a mere gratuity, for no public body has authority to give away the money of other people in gratuities. Whatever is paid by the employer is earned by the employed. The employer either pays enough to the workman to enable him to provide for his own old age in the way that best pleases him; or pays him something less than that adequate wage, upon the understanding that the remainder is to be given by way of pension. This is so whether the pension is paid directly by the employer, or whether he passes through the formality of raising a fund to which the workman and the employer jointly contribute. There is no difference in principle between the contribution of the workman and the contribution of the employer. Both are really contributions by the workman; that is, both are equally portions of the agreed remuneration for his labour. That principle is understood and acted upon in the Civil Service. The formality of deducting a contribution from salaries is dispensed with, and the state pays the whole of the pension according to a fixed scale. The principle applies equally to a private employer. He has no fund out of which to pay gratuities. The competition of other employers would soon deprive him of it if he had.

It is nevertheless not unusual for employers to seek the sanction of parliament to clauses by which they claim for themselves the whole control of the pension fund, however raised, and the right to grant or withhold pensions at their pleasure. They also claim the right to retain the employer's contribution to the fund, and in some cases also the men's contribution as well, in the case of a man retiring from their service or being dismissed before the pensionable age. As we have seen that there is no difference in principle between the two contributions, these are provisions which are unjust in themselves, and to which the legislature should not consent.

It is easy to see, on the other hand, that an arrangement of the kind would commend itself to the employer, as giving him security for the continued services and for the good behaviour of the employed. Where it is entered into as a free contract between the two parties, it may even be advantageous to the well-conducted workman, as enabling him to obtain better pay as an equivalent for the concession he makes; but that is not a ground upon which the legislature should consent to an enactment of a compulsory kind. There is a possible exception in the case of a dismissal arising from conduct of a fraudulent character by which the employer has suffered loss, in which it might not be unjust to apply the share of the employed in the pension fund towards meeting such loss.

There are two points which should be considered. The first is, that where a workman has no contract with his employer for a pension, it is because the rate of wages which he has agreed to accept and his employer to give is offered and taken as the full value of his services, including such provision for the future as is necessary to cover the waste of wage-earning power that the workman has to suffer. He therefore accepts for himself the responsibility of providing for his own old age. If he had stipulated with his employer for a pension, he would have had to accept lower wages. The question of "living wage" does not arise. He has fixed his own value upon that. The second is, that whether a workman has a contract with his employer for a pension or not, it rests with him to secure by other means the payment of a sum at death; as the whole equivalent of the deferred pay is included in the pension, which is calculated at a higher rate for the reason that it does not include any provision for a payment at death before the pensionable age.

Some interesting light on the granting of life-annuities in early times is thrown by a volume recently printed for the General Life Assurance Society of the Netherlands at Amsterdam, and presented to the members of the International Congress of Actuaries. In the communal archives of Tournai, one of the most ancient cities of Holland, and the seat of the Merovingian kings as far back as the fifth century, seven contracts for life-annuities have been discovered, dated 1228 and 1229, which have escaped the destruction that befell those archives shortly after, and are therefore probably only specimens of a much larger number of similar contracts that may have been entered into. By one of these documents, the Provosts, Jurors, Echevins, Electors, Maire, and all the Commune of Tournai acknowledge that they owe to John, son of William le Parcier, a burgess of Arras, 28 livres parisis of annual rente, to be paid to him as long as he shall have life in his body, on the festival of All Saints, at Arras, or in some other place at the same distance from Tournai, in a peaceful land, or at least in a sure place, indicated by the said John, acting in good faith; but if he dies before Elisabeth, daughter of Hubert le Parcier, half of the annuity shall be annulled, and the other half shall be paid to Elisabeth as long as she lives; but if John shall marry in a legitimate manner while Elisabeth is alive, he may substitute his legitimate wife for Elisabeth as the annuitant in respect of the half allowed to her as survivor. They also covenant, in case of default of payment of the annuity, to pay any expenses that John and Elisabeth may swear they have incurred, as well as the arrears; and in case John or Elisabeth should take the religious habit, still to pay the annuity. In some of the other policies, the local authorities bind themselves to submit to public excommunication by the bishop if they fail to fulfil their contract. Two similar contracts, dated 1273 and 1288, have been discovered in the archives of Ghent. The first was granted by St. John's Hospital to Heer Sanderse van den Boengaerde, securing him an annual rent of nine sous for his life, in consideration of his having ceded a farm to the hospital in perpetuity, as alms for the good of his soul. The other was granted by the echevins and community of the city of Ghent.

The grant by the religious house was similar to the corodies which the king or other founder of a monastery frequently reserved to himself for enabling a chaplain or other inmate to be maintained in the house during life or to obtain a pension out of its revenues. Such corodies were sometimes purchased by private persons; in which case it is probable that the monastery, like the hospital of St. Jean of Ghent, did not often get the worst of the bargain.

There is thus very ancient precedent for the system

of sale of life-annuities which the Commissioners for the Reduction of the National Debt have now carried on for many years. In the early part of their history the principles of annuity assurance were not so well known as at present, and the effect of an annuity in prolonging life was not fully appreciated. Mr. John Finlaison (who, by a rare felicity in the public service, has been succeeded in the office of actuary to the National Debt by his son and grandson) investigated this matter, and prepared tables on proper principles, so that these contracts are now as profitable to the community as they are convenient to the individuals who enter into them.

The Company of Mercers of the City of London passed through a curious experience in relation to annuity transactions. In the year 1698 the Rev. Dr. Assheton, rector of Beckenham, Kent, conceived a philanthropic scheme which was to relieve the wives of the clergy and of other professional men from all fear of pecuniary distress at the death of their husbands. An enthusiastic clergyman can generally get a hearing for any scheme with such an object; and Dr. Assheton found his willing audience in the general court of the Mercers' Company. His plan was this:—That for every £100 paid down to the company by a husband, the company should guarantee to the wife £30 a year for every year she survived him. As in those days nothing was known of the science of vital contingencies, for it will be recollected that the early insurance companies charged £5 per cent all round, irrespective of age, and that Necker granted annuities for life of 10 per cent in the same way, the preposterous nature of this contract was not seen through; and the company, which had recently spent large sums in rebuilding the

Royal Exchange, thought an opportunity of practical benevolence presented itself which would restore the capital expended. Deeds were drawn up by Sir Nathan Wright, afterwards Lord-keeper of the Great Seal, and Edward Northey, afterwards Attorney-general, for effecting these contracts and appropriating the income of the company's estates for the payment of the annuities as they should fall due, and were formally executed by the company on 4th October, 1699. For several years the company received money under these contracts, but their improvident nature soon came to be seen. In January, 1709, an order was made that husbands above 45 years of age were not to be admitted if their wives were 15 years younger. In 1716 the annuities were reduced to 25 per cent for future contracts; in 1723, to 20 per cent; in 1740, to 15 per cent; and in 1745 the company found its position in the matter intolerable, and made proposals for determining the contracts and closing the business. Both the annuitants and the company appealed to Parliament, and their respective statements are very quaint documents. The matter ended in the company being allowed to raise funds by means of a lottery.

This interesting story may serve to show that it is not only the members of Friendly Societies who have had to learn by experience that contracts depending on the duration of life cannot safely be entered upon except in accordance with accurate scientific data. The skilled actuary may be thought to be a very troublesome person, but some attention to his advice at the inception of a scheme may save a great deal of disappointment and embarrassment a long time after.

The Loan Societies Acts of 1835 and 1840 were, it would seem, intended to promote societies of a semicharitable type, granting debentures to the people who contributed the funds, and taking repayment on easy terms from borrowers for the small sums lent to them. The amount to be lent to each borrower is not to exceed £15, and no borrower is to have a second loan until the first one is repaid. A variety of schemes are provided in the schedule to the Act, in which, by a careful adjustment of the date of the first instalments and of the amount of each instalment with the amount to be deducted from interest, it is arranged that the interest payable on the loan should be equivalent to 12 per cent per annum. Thus, taking the most popular arrangement, that of repayment by instalments of 6*d.* in the £ per week in 40 weeks, it is provided that the first payment is not to be made until the 16th day after the loan, and that the interest to be deducted is not to exceed 1*s.* in the £. If, however, the rate of repayment selected were 1*s.* per £ per week, then the amount to be deducted for interest would be only 8*d.* per £, and the first repayment would not be due until the 35th day. The variety of schemes may be indefinitely increased by pushing backward or forward the date of first payment, and forward or backward the amount of interest, at the rate of 14 days for every 1*d.* per £ interest. As if all these options might not be sufficient, it was provided that a society might adopt any scheme which the Actuary to the National Debt might certify to be equivalent; and several such certificates have been granted. As the rate of interest adopted in these calculations is higher than the rate which was legal at the time of the passing of the acts, it became necessary to exempt the Loan Societies from the operations of the Usury Acts. Those acts, however, have long since been repealed for many good reasons, among which the easiness with which they could be evaded, the encouragement they give to breach of contract, and the difficulties they place in the way of the honest borrower, are not the least in importance. Though not liable to the penalties of the Usury Laws, the societies were expressly prohibited from charging any borrower, directly or indirectly, by way of fine, or purchase of books, papers, or other things, or in any other way, more than the amount allowed for interest by the scheme adopted. They were permitted to charge a sum not exceeding 1*s*. 6*d*. for each loan as an inquiry fee, but this 1*s*. 6*d*. was to be in full of all demands for inquiry, for executing the note, for the pass-book, and for all other charges.

The semi-benevolent Loan Societies have almost wholly died out, and their places have been taken by the Friends of Labour Loan Societies. These are, as far as possible, mutual societies, making little or no distinction between borrower and lender. In some, indeed, it is required that every member should become a borrower. Their place has been to some extent occupied by the specially authorized Loan Societies, and their business has decreased, especially of late years; but every year new societies are formed under the Act of 1840, and they appear still to fulfil a public demand. Thus in the three years 1892 to 1895, the number of societies has diminished from 358 to 341, the number of members from 40,492 to 37,711, the total amount due to depositors and shareholders from £290,582 to £265,869, and the number of borrowers from 68,823, to 61,724.

Though the societies are strictly tied down to a prescribed rate of interest, yet as that rate is so liberal as to be equivalent to 12 per cent per annum, it has been found to be an attraction to investors. Thus, though of the whole 341 societies, only 72 have more than £10 per member, 17 have more than £100 per member. A society at Bradford, with only four members, has a capital of £4696. This is really a partnership of small capitalists. The society having the largest number of members is one in Pimlico, with 870. The Loan Societies Act does not extend to Scotland or Ireland.

One side of the transactions of these societies which has a certain painful kind of interest is the measures which they are under the necessity of taking to recover the money they lend. In the year 1895, 2947 summonses were issued to recover £6554, and £4777 was recovered by this means. The number of distress warrants that had to be issued was 373. Dividing the societies into two groups, according to the amount of capital per member, we find that in the 17 societies of small capitalists where each member on the average has £300 in the funds, the summonses and distress warrants were nearly three times as many, compared with the amount of money in circulation, as the summonses and distress warrants issued by the 324 societies in the aggregate of which each member has on the average a capital of £6 only. It would seem therefore that the society of small capitalists presses more hardly upon the borrower than the mutual society does.

The mutual societies mainly exist in the south of England: Middlesex, Surrey, and Hampshire claiming the greatest number. The small capitalist societies belong principally to the north. The legislation relating to Loan Societies is of an antiquated type, but the circumstance that it is still put in operation seems to show that they exercise a useful function. As in all societies where the individual interest is too small to ensure adequate supervision, they are liable to loss by the peculation of officials. There is no reason to think that they bear hardly on borrowers, and, speaking generally, it may be assumed that the investing member suffers more and is more deserving of sympathy than the borrower, who pays a rate of interest which, though liberal, is not more than enough to produce the necessary reserve against default.

Societies for the promotion of literature, science, and the fine arts are hardly to be ranked with Provident Societies; yet they contribute so largely to the individual welfare of those in all classes of life who avail themselves of their benefits that it is not altogether without reason that the Registrar of Friendly Societies has been entrusted with the duty of certifying that they are entitled to the benefit of exemption from local rates which is conferred upon them by an Act passed in 1843, in the session of the sixth and seventh years of Her Majesty's reign; and we may with the same good reason be permitted to refer to them here. The conditions under which the certificate is to be granted are:—

1. That the body applying is a society.
2. That it is wholly or in part supported by annual voluntary contributions, which means contributions of money.
3. That it is exclusively for purposes of literature, science, and the fine arts.
4. That by its rules it may not make any dividend, gift, division, or bonus in money unto or between any of its members.

Several cases either of granting or of refusal of certificate under this Act have come to be reviewed in the law-courts, and the tendency of most of the decisions has been to narrow the benefits of the Act. It has been held that the purpose of education, though mainly directed to the subjects enumerated, is not within the Act; that where a scientific society has in view the professional advancement of its members, it is not entitled to a certificate; and that the expression, voluntary contributions, is to be interpreted to mean contributions in respect of which no return in kind is to be made. The recent decision of the Court of Appeal in favour of the Royal College of Music is possibly an indication of a tendency in the direction of a more liberal construction of the statute. A considerable number of Free Libraries in various parts of the country have brought themselves within its terms and obtained certificates; and as their main, though not their only, means of support is a contribution from the rates, there appears to be no good reason why they should not be exempted from payment of rates. An essential condition of the exemption is, however, that they should be, in part at least, supported by voluntary contributions of money.

Chapter XV.

Industrial Welfare.

We now proceed to consider what has been the effect of all these provident movements upon industrial welfare during the Victorian era. We have seen that in the earlier part of that era Trades-unions were held to be unlawful. We find them now not certainly covering the whole field of labour, skilled or unskilled, nor, in fact, covering more than a fractional part of it; not accumulating large funds, and yet not shrinking from pledging all the funds they have on the doubtful issue of a strenuous conflict; nevertheless exercising a powerful influence on both parties in the state, and recognized as representatives of the interests of labour. We find they have a wonderful faculty of recovering after a defeat, and great resources in the heroic self-denial of their members. Have not these bodies contributed to the welfare of the industrial community? The superficial observer takes note of the loss of wages suffered during a prolonged strike, of the sufferings caused by it to the workmen and their wives and children, of the disadvantage to the community that arises when capital invested in a large plant lies idle and production is suspended, and of the possibility that trade is diverted to other countries, and concludes that Trades-unions are pestilent institutions, which our ancestors were right in suppressing, and that it is a pity we cannot do the same. The more accurate thinker takes note rather of the normal operation of Trades-unions in securing by peaceable means the concession of their rights to the great mass of workmen, in creating a body of thoughtful and well-informed men who know when the condition of the labour market justifies them in urging a claim and when it would be folly to do so, and in providing for workmen, by means of combination, the opportunity of meeting their employers on equal terms. For one dispute that is brought to the stern decision of a strike, there are many that are settled by peaceful conference. Though, in general, the rough test of the rightfulness of a strike is its success, it is not every strike that is the fault of the workmen, and not every unsuccessful strike that leaves them wholly defeated.

We have also seen great and continuous increase in the operations of Friendly Societies, especially of that highly-organized class called the affiliated orders. The amount of the increase is difficult to ascertain precisely; but all the indications that can be obtained show that it has been progressive in a marked degree. In measuring the extent to which they have contributed to industrial welfare, we observe, in the first place, not so much the large amount of capital they have accumulated, as the amount which they have distributed. In that point of view, any errors of calculation of which they may have been guilty become immaterial—those errors have not affected the application of the funds, which have all gone to the relief of sickness or distress. One member or another may have received more sick pay than is the mathematical equivalent of the contributions he made, and may accordingly have left behind, in the funds, an insufficient provision for those who have not yet been sick; but so far as he himself is concerned, he has not received more than he wanted. Every penny the societies have spent has been spent beneficially, even if better knowledge would have distributed the benefits in a more equitable manner. No estimate of the amount thus distributed in sixty years would be trustworthy; and we have had occasion to use so many big figures upon authentic data, that any big figures we might employ upon hypothesis would fail in effect: but the reader may imagine for himself the vast sums that have been distributed by these voluntary and mutual societies among their sick and distressed members. As to the present financial circumstances of these societies, we have written so fully and so plainly that it is not necessary here to emphasize the fact that they are essential elements in the security and prosperity of those who belong to them.

The social side of Friendly Society work has always been one of its attractions. The insurance side of it has, as we have seen, largely developed out of the social side. As time has gone on, it has gradually become relatively more and more important, but has not yet extinguished, and probably never will extinguish, the social element. This has a great value in accustoming men to the observance of the requirements of courtesy and mutual consideration, in promoting well-ordered discussion and debate, in training them in the knowledge of affairs, and in many other ways.

The institution of Working-men's Clubs, in which no insurance element enters, has the same advantages. We have entered upon these fully in a previous chapter, and have also dealt with some drawbacks incidental to the constitution of these clubs. If we contrast the elements of social life which are embodied in these clubs with such social amenities as were open to the working-man before these clubs existed, which in general centred in the smoking-room of the village inn, or of the tavern in towns, we shall see that by the unpretending efforts of the Working-men's Clubs a considerable addition to the welfare of the industrial classes has been quietly achieved.

The other bodies to which the provisions of the Friendly Societies Act extend represent methods of meeting various requirements of civil life by the application of the fruitful principle of free and self-governing combination, and carry to a greater or smaller number of people benefits and facilities which they appreciate as suited to their particular wants. In this point of view they are all signs of progress, and indications that the power of association is more and more found to be applicable and advantageous.

The Industrial and Provident Societies have contributed to the improvement of the condition of their members by enabling them to supply themselves with good and cheap food, and other necessaries of life; by raising their standard of enjoyment; by the profitable investment of their savings; and by measures of a directly educational kind. In the productive department they have provided employment for their members at fair rates, and placed on the market trustworthy and well-made commodities. The great wholesale societies have formed themselves into a centre of the movement, chartered a fleet of ships, built vast manufactories, established a system of credit and of supervision, to the great advantage of the smaller societies, and contributed to the promotion of the national welfare. The benefits of the co-operative system have extended far beyond the circle of the members, not merely by the establishment of large stores dealing with particular classes of the public, such as civil servants and officers in the army and navy, but more especially by the blow they have dealt to the system of obtaining credit from traders by private individuals. The general rule of these stores being to require payment in cash, and to sell the commodities dealt with at cash prices, persons who are able to pay ready money have learnt that it is not worth their while to pay the prices which traders who give credit are bound to exact in order to get interest for their money, and meet the losses arising from debtors who cannot or will not pay. The result of the competition between cash stores and credit dealers has thus been to compel the tradesmen to lower their prices, and for that purpose to restrict within narrower bounds the practice of giving credit to individuals, to the great benefit of themselves and their customers.

Building Societies and other organizations that have done the like work are also to be credited with having greatly contributed to industrial welfare. At a conference recently held by the Building Societies Association at Bradford, it was stated by a local resident that nine out of ten of the houses in that town have been built by the aid of Building Societies. If this computation be correct, it is probable that Leeds, Rochdale, Oldham, and other towns would not be far behind.

The large sums deposited in Savings-banks, or invested through their means, indicate that the owners possess a surplus after providing themselves with the necessaries of life. So far as the facilities they offer for saving, and the attraction afforded by the rate of interest, have operated to induce persons to save who would not otherwise have done so, they have tended to the creation of wealth; but it is not to be supposed that all the vast sums deposited are thus to be accounted for. Some no doubt would have been saved if no Savings-banks had existed, even if the savings had been placed idly away in an old stocking or a battered teapot. Savings-banks, moreover, are open to the public generally, and it is not therefore to be assumed that all the deposits belong to the industrial classes. The Postmaster-general made an effort in the year 1896–97 to determine by what classes of the community the Post-office Savings-bank was chiefly used. The method he adopted was to record for a period of three months the occupations of all new depositors, as furnished by themselves on opening their accounts. Assuming these to be fairly typical of the whole number, the result would be that for every 10,000 depositors, 155 belong to the professional class, 281 are officials, 101 engaged in education, 388 in commercial pursuits, 183 in the agricultural and fishing industries, 1843 in other industrial occupations, 296 in railways, shipping, and transport, 814 are tradesmen and their assistants, 861 domestic servants, 37 not capable of being grouped otherwise than as miscellaneous, and 5041 described as married women, spinsters, widows, and children. As the last item forms more than one-half of the whole, it will be seen that the materials for classification are imperfect. The Postmaster-general adds that women and children of all ranks, including those so described, are believed to be 6059 in every 10,000 of the total number of depositors.

To sum up. We have seen that the Trade-unions possess £2,138,296, the Friendly Societies £25,408,253, the Working-men Clubs £107,938, other societies under the Friendly Societies Acts £535,301, the Industrial and Provident Societies £28,451,328, the Building Societies £56,397,457, the Trustee Savings-banks £53,699,532, the Post-office Savings-bank £108,098,641, the Railway Savings-banks £3,124,069, the Loan Societies £265,869. We have thus an aggregate of £277,955,815 independent of the annuities and assurances granted by the National Debt Commissioners—altogether, not far short of 300 millions of money accumulated in these various institutions. We have endeavoured under each head fairly to state the considerations which, on one side and the other, are to be borne in mind in estimating the effect of the several movements; and we cannot resist the conclusion that, after every allowance has been made, there has been throughout the Victorian era an extension of the principles and methods of Provident Societies that is beyond comparison greater than in any previous time in history, and has been the instrument of widespread moral and material benefit, especially to that section of the community which has been growing steadily in political importance, and is comprehended in the expression, "the industrial population". Though much may still remain to be desired, it cannot be doubted that their condition has greatly improved during the period under observation.

More direct evidence is available. Mr. Ludlow was asked in 1892 to give the Royal Commission on Labour his general impression as to the changes in the condition of the working-classes during the long time in which he had made a careful study of it. He said, "I think the condition of the working-class has changed immensely, but not so much, I am happy to say, as the change in public opinion on the subjects relating to that class. I find now that boys and girls fresh from school are at a point of advancement in relation to this question which in 1848 we could not bring grown-up people to, and were considered heretics and revolutionists for trying to bring them to. I think the change in public opinion on that subject has been something perfectly marvellous. I cannot express it sufficiently. The working-class also has developed enormously in intellectual acquirements and habits of business and largeness of outlook, though perhaps they have lost a little of that enthusiasm and spirit of generous aspiration which I think distinguished my working-men friends of the earlier days. Now the black spots in the country may, I think, almost be counted on the fingers. In former days it was very nearly all black with but few white spots."

In 1867 Mr. Ludlow published, in association with the late Mr. Lloyd Jones, a work on the *Progress of the*

Working-classes since 1832. That date was selected with relation to the passing of the Reform Bill, but it is sufficiently near the date of the commencement of the Victorian era to warrant us in treating the progress he recorded as marking the half-way house between that time and the present. In Part I. of the work, Mr. Lloyd Jones described, in the main from personal knowledge, the condition of the working-class in 1832. He quoted the testimony of Sir J. P. Kay Shuttleworth as to the long hours of labour, the insufficient and unwholesome food, the half-savage domestic habits, the unwholesome conditions of life of the Manchester cotton workers. The children then employed in all the principal branches of manufacture throughout the kingdom worked during the same number of hours as the adults. They began to work in some rare instances at five years old—the greatest number were under nine. The effects were deterioration of the physical constitution, deformity and disease, and the partial or entire exclusion from the means of obtaining adequate education and acquiring useful habits. The Factory Acts belonging to the early portion of the Victorian era to some extent stopped overwork, and brought an educational machinery into operation; but in 1843 it was reported that in the area of eight miles by four comprising the boroughs of Oldham and Ashton, for a population of 105,000 there was not a single public day-school for the children of the humbler ranks. The factory schools which the children were required to attend for two hours in the day were insufficient, and such education as was given was derived from the Sunday-school. As to the amusements of the masses, Mr. Lloyd Jones drew an equally unfavourable picture:—"Sullen, silent work alternated with noisy, drunken riot; and Easter and Whitsuntide debauches, with an occasional outbreak during some favourite wakes, rounded the whole life of the factory worker".

The ordinary artisan of the workshop was a far different man. He had time for study when inclined, and as a rule had received more education. Still, the workshop of those days was by no means the most desirable school for a youth to commence the active duties of life in. In the highest-paid trades, work was not to be had on a Monday from the artisan; many men only began their week on the Thursday. There were some grave men devoted to intellectual pursuits, but they were exceptional. Mr. Lloyd Jones tells a story of one, an enthusiastic entomologist, coming to work after an absence of several days, and explaining the cause of it by saying that he had been attending his own funeral, and making merry over his departure from the world. The fact was, he had gone to the officers of his Burial Club, and compounded his future claims for cash down, which he had spent in making himself jolly. It was with the more sober and thoughtful artisans that the agitation for the Short-time Bill began. They saw and felt much sooner than the factory workers themselves what a curse the system as it then existed was, and it was long before those most directly interested in the agitation could be brought to take much concern in it. A friend of Mr. Lloyd Jones told him of having gone to speak at a short-time meeting at a village near Manchester; he found himself, as he neared the spot, in the midst of a crowd of factory operatives going in the same direction. Delighted, he said to one of them, "We shall have a good meeting in favour of the Short-time Bill". "Nay," shouted the man, "it's nobbut a dog-fight."

The Trade-unions of that day, Mr. Lloyd Jones

describes as "generally ill-managed, secret in their rules and deliberations, and too often tyrannical in their proceedings. In nearly all of them there was a tendency to violence." He knew personally two men belonging to different trades who had been rendered at different times totally blind by having vitriol thrown in their faces by men on strike. Knobsticks, as men who worked under price were called, were maltreated and sometimes murdered. Apart from the unions, great damage was done by riotous mobs. He himself was present "during the destruction by fire of one of the Manchester factories. The burning building was surrounded by thousands of excited people, whose faces, reddened by the ascending flames, expressed fierce and savage joy. As the fire forced its way from floor to floor, darting through the long rows of windows, cries of exultation were shouted by the crowd; and when, finally, bursting through the roof, it went roaring into the heavens, the maddened multitude danced with delight, shouting and clapping their hands as in uncontrollable thankfulness for a great triumph."

Mr. Ludlow, in a note appended to the work, which was written before Trades-unions were legalized, referred to the Broadhead case in Sheffield. He said, "what we see is but the last flickering out, not the first outbreak of a baleful flame. There is no novelty in any of the outrages; the only novelty is the knowing all about them. At the time when the combination laws were repealed they were common to many trades and towns, instead of being confined to a few trades in one or two towns; they have simply lingered in these since the time when every trade society was an illegal combination, and when personal violence was almost the only agency that could be employed to enforce the behests of committees. Frightful as these revelations are . . . they show that the habit of exclusively considering the class interest of the worker may beget a temper as reckless, as deadly, as fiendish as the religious fanaticism of a sect of assassins."

We have quoted freely from this excellent work, long since out of print, and now rarely met with, on account of both the intrinsic interest and the unimpeachable authority of the statements. Mr. Ludlow traces to the Factories Act, the Mines Act, and a number of other statutes relating to industrial occupations, the great amelioration in some of the conditions of industrial life which had already taken place when he wrote; and the operation of those legislative measures has been continued and strengthened to the present day. The inspection has become more and more efficient. The excellent measure of appointing women inspectors of factories has only recently been adopted. If factory legislation is necessary for men, who ought to be able to help themselves, how much more is it obligatory upon the legislature to do all that can be done to help women and children who cannot help themselves. In carrying out the provisions of the Factories Acts, as well as in the fulfilment of the functions of guardian of the poor, the services of accomplished and enlightened women cannot but be of the highest possible value.

Another cause to which Mr. Ludlow rightly attributes much of the progress of the working-classes is the recognition by the state of education as an object of national policy. The first vote of £30,000 for public elementary education in Great Britain occurs in the Appropriation Act of the 3rd and 4th Vict., 11th August, 1840; and the vote of the next year, 1841, was even less

—only £15,000. The grant for the session of 1886, when Mr. Ludlow wrote, was £694,530. The grant for the session of 1898, moved by Sir John Gorst in a memorable speech, is £4,920,175. Great as is this expenditure out of national funds, it has to be supplemented by contributions of the ratepayers where board schools exist, and by voluntary contributions where voluntary schools only exist.

Until the year 1870, a married woman could hold no property of her own. All that she possessed belonged in law to her husband, and he could do with it what he willed. The wealthy classes sought to remedy this wrong by the system of marriage settlements. The property intended to be secured to the wife, free from her husband's control, was legally vested in trustees for her benefit. This remedy was not available for the poor. The drunken and worthless husband of an industrious woman had the absolute right to every penny she earned. If she placed her earnings in a Savings-bank, her receipt would be a good discharge to the trustees, but only so long as her husband did not claim the money. The records of the earlier disputes in relation to Savings-banks deposits are full of pathetic instances in which poor women availed themselves of every possible expedient to prevent their husband getting scent of the fact that they had saved money. The Act of 1870 directed that the wages and earnings of any married woman, gained after its passing, in an employment, occupation, or trade carried on by her separately from her husband, and any property acquired by her through the exercise of any literary, artistic, or scientific skill, should be taken to be property held and settled to her separate use, independent of her husband, and it made provision that deposits in Savings-banks, property in the funds, shares in companies, and benefits in Friendly and other societies, might also be so held. The Married Women's Property Act, 1882, greatly extended these remedies, and gave to a married woman full powers of holding property without the intervention of trustees, and the absolute right to all earnings and property acquired by her from her own exertions, or devolving upon her; it also provided that the deposits, shares, and other benefits referred to in the previous Act should be deemed to be her separate property until the contrary be shown. Though the hard-working woman may still have to endure much at the hands of a bad husband, these statutes have been for her a charter of freedom, and are the concession of an act of justice which had been only too long delayed.

Mr. Ludlow points out that the Newspaper Act of 1836 commenced the emancipation of the newspaper press, which the acts for the removal of the taxes on knowledge have since carried out. As to the value of the newspaper press as an educational organ, the testimony of Mr. John Morley may be taken. He suggests that classes should be formed for the study of the daily paper, and shows that not a single issue of it ever appears which does not test and extend the knowledge of the best informed among us.

Other reforms—such as that by which working-men have been appointed to the justices' bench, elected members of municipal corporations, and of parliament itself—the abolition of the vexatious indirect taxation of a past day—the better provision for sanitation of towns, villages, and dwellings—have had an important share in promoting the welfare of the industrial population; but it remains as one of the great glories of the Victorian era, that, as we have attempted to show, that welfare has been established in a very large degree by the labours and the sacrifices of working-men themselves, and by the wise and judicious legislation which has permitted and encouraged their endeavours in the direction of self-help. Those who have thus been able "to cheer and aid, in some ennobling cause, their fellow-men" have not lived in vain.

Index.

Printed in Dunstable, United Kingdom

91221355R00131